THE UNITED STATES–JAPAN ECONOMIC PROBLEM

POLICY ANALYSES IN INTERNATIONAL ECONOMICS 13

THE UNITED STATES–JAPAN ECONOMIC PROBLEM

C. Fred Bergsten
William R. Cline

92-1368

INSTITUTE FOR INTERNATIONAL ECONOMICS
WASHINGTON, DC
OCTOBER 1985. Revised JANUARY 1987

C. Fred Bergsten is Director of the Institute for International Economics. He was formerly Assistant Secretary of the Treasury for International Affairs; Assistant for International Economic Affairs to the National Security Council; and a Senior Associate at the Carnegie Endowment for International Peace, The Brookings Institution, and Council on Foreign Relations.

William R. Cline is a Senior Fellow at the Institute for International Economics. He was formerly a Senior Fellow at The Brookings Institution; Deputy Director for Development and Trade Research at the US Treasury Department; Ford Foundation Visiting Professor at the Instituto de Planejamento Econômico e Social Aplicado (IPEA) in Brazil; and Assistant Professor at Princeton University.

The authors are grateful to the following individuals for helpful comments: Bela Balassa, Richard N. Cooper, I.M. Destler, Reginald H. Jones, Roger M. Kubarych, Robert Z. Lawrence, Marc Noland, Hirohiko Okumura, Hugh Patrick, and Gary R. Saxonhouse, as well as experts in the US Department of Commerce and Office of the US Trade Representative.

The authors thank Ron Friedman for research assistance and Maurice Feller and Debbie McGuire who typed this manuscript.   C.F.B. and W.R.C.

Library of Congress Catalog Card Number 86-83417

ISBN 0-88132-060-9

Contents

TEXT FIGURES

Preface

The economic conflict between the United States and Japan had, by late 1985, become one of the most critical issues facing the two countries and the world economy as a whole. Their global imbalances had soared to levels of surplus (Japan) and deficit (the United States) far beyond anything ever before recorded by industrial countries, as had the bilateral gap between them. One result was an enormous increase in pressure for trade restrictions against Japan, with potentially severe consequences for the global trading regime. Continued failure to resolve the problem threatened severe economic costs to both countries, overall relations between them, and the functioning of the international economic system.

Yet much of the debate on the issue appeared to miss, or ignore, several vitally important points. There was a failure to distinguish between the trade *imbalances*, which result primarily from exchange rate misalignment and underlying macroeconomic phenomena, and the trade *policy* problem, which focuses on individual industries and emphasizes such policy tools as tariffs and import quotas. There was no quantitative analysis of the significance of Japanese trade barriers or, despite the widespread calls for "reciprocity," how they compared with American trade barriers. There seemed to be no clear sense of priorities: did the needed corrections lie primarily with the fundamental structures of the two countries, with their macroeconomic policies, or with their approaches to particular sectors and even individual products? What is *meant* by "balance" in the economic relationship between the United States and Japan?

This study attempts to answer these and other key analytical questions underlying the US-Japan economic conflict, and the present second edition adds a postscript which updates some of the key conclusions through 1986. On the basis of these analyses, the study recommends a series of policy actions for both countries through which they could address the problem more effectively. In doing so, the authors draw on several other studies recently published by the Institute, in particular: *The Exchange Rate System* by John Williamson (revised, June 1985), *Deficits and the Dollar: The World*

Economy at Risk by Stephen Marris (December 1985), *The Yen/Dollar Agreement: Liberalizing Japanese Capital Markets* by Jeffrey A. Frankel (December 1984), and *Trading for Growth: The Next Round of Trade Negotiations* by Gary Clyde Hufbauer and Jeffrey J. Schott (September 1985).

In conducting their research, the authors were greatly assisted by comments received on an early draft at a discussion meeting held at the Institute on July 10, 1985, and conveyed subsequent to that meeting, by a large number of governmental, corporate, academic, and other experts. The study was also informed by the discussions at several meetings of the United States–Japan Consultative Group on International Monetary Affairs, a small group of leading American and Japanese economists sponsored by the US–Japan Foundation (which provided partial support for this study) and chaired by the Institute.

The Institute for International Economics is a private, nonprofit research institution for the study and discussion of international economic issues. Its purpose is to analyze important topics in this area of public policy, and to develop and communicate practical new approaches for dealing with them. The Institute is completely nonpartisan.

The Institute was created in November 1981 through a generous funding commitment from the German Marshall Fund of the United States. Substantial support is now also being provided by a number of other private foundations and corporations.

The Board of Directors bears overall responsibility for the Institute and gives general guidance and approval to its research program—including identification of topics that are likely to become important to international economic policymakers over the medium run (generally, one to three years) and which thus should be addressed by the Institute. The Director of the Institute, working closely with the staff and outside Advisory Committee, is responsible for the development of particular projects and makes the final decision to publish an individual study.

The Institute hopes that its studies and other activities will contribute to building a stronger foundation for international economic policy around the world. Comments as to how it can best do so are invited from readers of these publications.

C. FRED BERGSTEN
Director
January 1987

x

1 Introduction

The current economic imbalance between the United States and Japan has produced one of the most serious crises to face the international trading system, and the world economy as a whole, in the postwar period. The huge American deficit and Japanese surplus are having major effects on production, employment, and other key economic variables in both countries. The pressures in the Congress and the US business community to adopt extensive new trade actions against Japan are enormous; if pursued, some of these actions could destroy much of what remains of the General Agreement on Tariffs and Trade (GATT) system which has contributed so significantly to postwar prosperity. The conflict could also turn into the most serious crisis in the overall relationship between the two countries since the war, with profound implications for the security of the entire Pacific area. The purpose of this study is to improve understanding of the problem, to suggest remedies to deal with it effectively, and to help avert systemic breakdown as a result of inadequate or inappropriate policy responses.

The magnitude of the imbalance has become enormous. The United States ran a deficit of over $100 billion in its global current account (trade in goods and services) in 1984, and that number will probably rise to at least $125 billion this year. Japan ran a current account surplus of $36 billion last year, which will probably rise to about $50 billion for 1985. The bilateral trade imbalance in Japan's favor was about $37 billion in 1984, and is expected to hit $45 billion to $50 billion in 1985.

These imbalances may well grow further before lasting correction can be achieved. If the dollar were to remain at the level of the end of September 1985, after the initial results of the intervention initiative launched by the Group of Five on September 22 (a trade-weighted decline of about 6 percent including a move of about 10 percent against the yen), the US current account deficit would continue rising to over $250 billion annually by 1990 (and the

1

United States would then be a net debtor country in excess of $1 trillion).[1] And even if this correction were to proceed far enough to reach the level needed for lasting equilibrium, the American current account would probably deteriorate further, at least into early 1986, barring a sharp domestic recession. It could not possibly approach balance until 1987 in light of the time lags from currency adjustment to changes in trade flows and the sheer magnitude of the deficit now.

In Japan, such respected analysts as the Industrial Bank of Japan and Nomura Research Institute estimate that, even with sizable appreciation of the yen, Japan will continue to run current account surpluses averaging about $50 billion annually throughout the 1980s and will become a net creditor country of $500 billion by the early 1990s.[2] Hence, it will take some time before the two countries' imbalances can return to previous or "acceptable" levels. In the short run, some reversal of the enormous deterioration that has been occurring since 1980–81 is the best that can be expected.

In essence, the external positions of the two largest economies in the world have been headed in opposite directions at an extremely rapid pace. Indeed, no country has ever run deficits of the magnitude now being experienced by the United States—and, aside from Saudi Arabia for a year or two after the second oil shock, no country has ever run surpluses like those of contemporary Japan. Not surprisingly, the bilateral imbalance between the two countries has soared. Equally unsurprisingly, the stability of the entire world economy is threatened by the possible repercussions from these disequilibria.

The US-Japan economic relationship is critical to both countries. Their integration through trade considerably exceeds that between either country and its other trading partners. In trade among industrial countries, the United States supplied 53.4 percent of Japan's imports in 1984 and Japan provided 30.9 percent of US imports. In contrast, the United States supplied only 20.1 percent of the imports of all other industrial countries, and Japan only 5.9

---

1. Even assuming slower economic growth in the United States than in the rest of the world, which would have a favorable effect on the US current account. Stephen Marris, *Deficits and the Dollar: The World Economy at Risk*, POLICY ANALYSES IN INTERNATIONAL ECONOMICS 14 (Washington: Institute for International Economics, December 1985).

2. Industrial Bank of Japan, *Quarterly Review* (January–March 1984), and Nomura Research Institute, "A Long-Term Outlook for the Japanese Economy (Fiscal 1984 to 1995)," Tokyo, 26 August 1985.

percent.[3] Where economic integration is proportionately so intense, and so large in absolute magnitudes, temporary imbalances may easily generate economic and political problems. Recognition of close de facto economic integration, which now includes capital markets as well as trade, highlights the importance to both the United States and Japan of resolving their economic conflicts in a positive way rather than by economic rupture.

The current "trade problem" has a number of dimensions. There are traditional problems of *trade policy* which involve questions of market access, fairness of national practices, and standard protectionism. These issues now focus particularly on Japan and relate to US exports to Japan (for example, telecommunications equipment), Japanese penetration of the American market (for example, automobiles), and global competition between the two economic superpowers (for example, computers and semiconductors). However, American trade policies, both import restraints and export controls (for example, on Alaskan oil), also affect both sides of the trade balance and must be considered in any comprehensive assessment of the problem.

There are also major issues of a *monetary and macroeconomic nature* in both countries. The sharp growth in the US budget deficit is a central element in the US trade deficit, for example. By contrast, Japan has been substantially reducing its budget deficit. The opposite directions of these national policies have contributed importantly to the trade imbalance.

Finally, *structural elements* of each society contribute to their external imbalances. At the macroeconomic level, the United States has an extremely low rate of national savings by international standards, and Japan has an extremely high rate. At the microeconomic level, Japan's *keiretsu* system of industry conglomerates tends to discriminate against nongroup (including foreign) suppliers, and for their part, many American companies simply have not made the effort necessary to penetrate the Japanese market.[4]

Conceptually, the problem thus can be divided into eight parts. In each country, there are both structural and policy elements. Both the structural and policy components include macroeconomic and microeconomic dimen-

---

3. Calculated from International Monetary Fund, *Direction of Trade Statistics Yearbook 1985*. Note that Japan's low share in the markets of other industrial countries indicates a greater Japanese dependency on the US market than vice versa.

4. Bruce R. Scott, "US Competitiveness: Concepts, Performance, and Implications," in *US Competitiveness in the World Economy*, edited by Bruce R. Scott and George C. Lodge (Boston, Mass.: Harvard Business School Press, 1985), pp. 13–70, notes that "a growing body of case study evidence supports this poor management theory . . ."

FIGURE 1.1 **Elements involved in trade surplus of Japan**

	Illustrative List	
	Structural	*Policy*
Macroeconomic	High savings rate	Sharp decline in budget deficits
Microeconomic	*Keiretsu* system	Industry targeting

sions. Figures 1.1 and 1.2 depict these matrices; an illustration of the type of issue involved appears in each cell. At this point, no weighting or relative importance should be attached to either the categories or the specific illustrations cited. It is clear from even a cursory glance, however, that problems exist in all eight cells.

The Macroeconomic Dimension

A key question is the degree to which each of these different problems is responsible for the ongoing trade friction between the two countries, and for its present escalation. How much is caused by specific competitive problems faced by *individual* industries? How much is due to the large and growing imbalances in macroeconomic forces affecting the *overall* trade balances of the two countries? How much of each type of problem is due to current policies, and how much to underlying structural features of the two societies? How do these various elements relate to each other?

The emphasis on these separate, but closely related, aspects of the problem has shifted back and forth over the past 15 years. However, most American and Japanese administrations have ultimately tried to address both. The Nixon administration, for example, initially emphasized textile imports from Japan but then in August 1971 turned to the overall trade balance, which, as now, comprised the global economic position of the United States rather than just relations with Japan, by ending the convertibility of foreign official dollar balances into gold and applying an import surcharge. The Carter administration tried to blend the two areas, pushing on beef and citrus and other specific sectors toward the Strauss–Ushiba Agreement of 1978 but focusing both initially and ultimately on the exchange rate and macroeconomic issues

FIGURE 1.2   **Elements involved in US trade deficit**

	Illustrative List	
	Structural	*Policy*
Macroeconomic	Low savings rate	Sharp increase in budget deficits
Microeconomic	Inadequate corporate efforts to penetrate Japanese market	Export controls (soybeans, Alaskan oil)

(notably at the Bonn summit in mid-1978 and its dollar defense program in late 1978 and 1979). The current administration emphasized the exchange rate at the Reagan-Nakasone summit in November 1983, but turned attention to specific sectors at the follow-up summit in January 1985 and subsequent Market-Oriented Sector-Specific (MOSS) negotiations before returning to the currency dimension in September 1985.

Our reading of both the current situation and the relevant history suggests that the sharp increase in the overall macroeconomic imbalances, to previously unimagined levels, represents by far the more significant issue in economic terms. We demonstrate in chapter 2 that virtually the entire growth in the bilateral imbalance, from about $12 billion in 1980 to almost $40 billion in 1984, can be explained by the onset of exchange rate misalignment and differences in economic growth rates. (Indeed there is little if any argument that Japan has been *increasing* its trade barriers or interventions.) Likewise, we conclude in chapter 3 that even a complete elimination of Japanese trade barriers, intangible as well as overt, would be likely to expand US exports in the near future by "only" $5 billion to $8 billion—a considerable sum in absolute terms, and of critical importance for trade policy (as discussed in chapter 4) but with only a modest impact on the overall imbalances. We thus find it hard to believe that individual sector problems—or even the cumulative effect of those that have surfaced—have triggered the present degree of tension. Explanation for the rapid *escalation* of tensions must lie elsewhere, notably at the macroeconomic level.

A close study of the evolution of US-Japan economic relations over the past two decades also reveals that frictions rise and fall in response to major changes in the exchange rate relationship between the dollar and yen, which in turn produce sharp swings in the global (and bilateral) trade balances of the countries.[5] The first severe outbreak of US-Japan economic conflict, which was a major element in triggering the Nixon-Connally import surcharge of 1971, occurred in the early 1970s when the dollar became overvalued in relation to the underlying American competitive position by 20 percent to 25 percent (as revealed, and corrected, by the devaluations of 1971 and 1973). The second outbreak, leading to the Strauss–Ushiba Agreement of 1978, followed the more modest dollar overvaluation of 1975–76.

By 1985, the dollar had become overvalued by 30 percent to 40 percent compared with the underlying competitive relationship between the United States and other major countries (on average).[6] Each rise of one percentage point in the real (inflation-adjusted) effective (trade-weighted) exchange rate of the dollar produces a deterioration of $2 billion to $3 billion in the global US trade balance, and each rise of one percentage point in the dollar-yen rate produces a deterioration of about $830 million vis-à-vis Japan (appendix B). Largely as a result of this historic currency misalignment, which relates importantly to the huge deficits in the US government budget, the United States has experienced an enormous deterioration in its trade balance, as described in chapter 2, not just with Japan but with every part of the world except the Organization of Petroleum Exporting Countries (OPEC, due to the falling price and volume of oil imports). To achieve equilibrium in the countries' global current accounts, the yen would have to strengthen to a range of at least 190 to 200 yen per dollar (from approximately 240 in 1984 and 250 in the first half of 1985, although after the joint interaction announcement by the Group of Five in late September, the rate had moved to the level of 215 to 220).[7]

---

5. This history is traced in C. Fred Bergsten, "What to Do About the U.S.-Japan Economic Conflict," *Foreign Affairs* (Summer 1982). A similar pattern in the relationship has been identified by Ryutaro Komiya and Miyako Suda, *Contemporary International Finance: Theory, History and Policy* (Tokyo: Nihon Keizai Shinbunsha, 1983).

6. Updated calculation to mid-September 1985 based on John Williamson, *The Exchange Rate System*, POLICY ANALYSES IN INTERNATIONAL ECONOMICS 5, 2d ed., rev. (Washington: Institute for International Economics, June 1985).

7. It should be noted that the yen has been weak only with respect to the dollar, and has indeed hit record *highs* against the European currencies over the past year. The trade-weighted average rate of the yen has *risen* by over 10 percent since 1980. See the discussion of "Exchange Rate Protection?" in chapter 3.

Japan's recent policies also have played a major role in generating the sharp rise in that country's external surpluses and the weakness of its currency against the dollar. The Japanese savings rate is now substantially in excess of domestic investment in Japan, largely because the government budget deficit has declined sharply and no longer absorbs the excess savings of the private sector, creating net capital outflows and a current account surplus.[8] In addition, the geographical distribution of Japanese investments is undergoing a policy-induced portfolio adjustment: Japanese savings were "bottled up" domestically to a considerable extent before the liberalization of exchange controls began in earnest in 1980 and accelerated rapidly in the past two years (under intense pressure from the US Treasury), but now flow abroad relatively freely.[9] As a result of these factors, along with the general "pull" into the dollar, caused primarily by high American interest rates and "safe-haven" considerations, long-term capital outflow from Japan has become massive, averaging over $5 billion a month and rising to over $8 billion a month in the summer of 1985, depressing the yen against the dollar and improving Japan's international competitive position against the United States. The Japanese saving-investment relationship is analyzed in detail in chapter 2.

The US-Japan disequilibrium thus has been magnified in recent years by the opposite directions of policy in the two countries. The United States has sharply increased its budget deficits which, along with a return of private investment to normal levels without any substantial increase in domestic savings, has raised interest rates and the international value of the dollar. Japan has been reducing its budget deficits, which until the early 1980s had

---

8. An excellent Japanese analysis can be found in Masaru Yoshitomi, "Japan's View of Current External Imbalances," in *Global Economic Imbalances,* edited by C. Fred Bergsten (Washington: Institute for International Economics, 1986). It suggests that the structural level of excess savings explains a current account surplus of about 1 percent to 1.5 percent of Japanese GNP, about one-third to one-half the present level.

9. Except for a continued "prudential limit" of 10 percent on the share of total investments by Japanese life insurance companies and pension trusts which can be held in foreign securities, and a continuing ban on most foreign investment by the postal savings system. See Hirohiko Okumura, "Japanese Portfolio Investments in Foreign Securities" (paper presented to the US-Japan Consultative Group on International Monetary Affairs, 25–26 April 1985, Hakone, Japan; processed).

soaked up most of the excess savings of the private sector, creating a sizable surplus of savings and pushing capital abroad.[10]

Moreover, recent policies adopted by the two countries which aim directly at international capital flows have made the yen-dollar problem worse. Japan's speeding of the liberalization of its capital markets, pushed by the United States during 1983–84, has increased capital *outflow* from Japan and thus has weakened the yen further.[11] American elimination of its withholding tax on interest payments to foreign investors in US Treasury securities, and Treasury's subsequent "tailoring" of its securities to the needs of such investors, further increased financial movements into the dollar (at least until Japan also removed its withholding tax) and intensified the trade problem.

Sector-Specific Issues

At the same time that macroeconomic factors seem to be dominant in increasing the overall imbalances being experienced by the United States and Japan, a perception of extensive "unfair" trade practices on the part of Japan looms exceedingly large in the political dimension of the problem. There clearly exists a widespread view, in Europe and elsewhere in Asia as well as in the United States, that Japan is "different": not only in the diligence of its people and underlying competitiveness of its economy, which are widely acknowledged and admired, but in the basic manner in which it relates to the rest of the world. Indeed, there was a "Japan problem," albeit to a much lesser degree, even when the aggregate imbalances were much smaller and exchange rates and other macroeconomic factors were much closer to equilibrium.

---

10. One specific aspect of these fiscal policy differences is worth notice because of its potential direct impact on the exchange rate: while the United States has cut corporate taxes and thus attracted capital in search of maximum profit opportunities, Japan has been raising its corporate taxes and thus reducing the appeal of investment (by Japanese as well as foreigners) in yen assets. Yukio Noguchi, "Tax Structure and Savings-Investment Balance" (paper presented to the US-Japan Consultative Group on International Monetary Affairs, 25–26 April 1985, Hakone, Japan; processed). Japanese corporate investment probably remains more lightly taxed than American corporate investment, however, and total private investment in Japan has remained strong through the first half of 1985.

11. Jeffrey A. Frankel, *The Yen/Dollar Agreement: Liberalizing Japanese Capital Markets,* POLICY ANALYSES IN INTERNATIONAL ECONOMICS 9 (Washington: Institute for International Economics, December 1984).

Part of the "specialness" of the Japan problem undoubtedly stems from the simple fact that it is a large country, the second most sizable economic power in the world. Part of the problem probably derives from its ability to challenge industry in America (and elsewhere) across the board, especially at the frontiers of high technology, which no other country can do. Part relates, no doubt, to the huge trade surpluses already discussed.

But this concern ranges far beyond the "normal" trade distortions such as tariffs, import quotas, and other visible nontariff barriers and export aids. It alleges that "Japan, Inc.," encompasses a unique brand of cooperation among government, industry, and labor which produces a formidable competitor unlike any other country. One specific manifestation of this alliance is said to be widespread "industry targeting," through which future "winners" are promoted and "losers" eased out in much more rapid and efficient manner than can be accomplished by the more traditional industrial policies employed in other countries—let alone the largely laissez-faire approach of the United States. In turn, such targeting is said to produce impenetrable import barriers (until Japan itself has developed world-class firms, and thus no longer needs the barriers) and powerful, if subtle, support for exports.

Other fundamental elements of Japanese society are also widely viewed as having the effect, if not the primary intent, of unfairly blocking access to the country's markets. The keiretsu system of social organization, under which some firms buy only from other firms in their "family group" and discriminate against all outsiders (Japanese as well as foreign), is one such practice. Another is the desire of powerful government bureaucrats, especially in the Ministry of International Trade and Industry (MITI), to maintain power and a plethora of lucrative postretirement positions in industry. Myriad lists of licensing, standards, testing, and certification requirements are widely thought to interrelate with these apparently deep-seated elements in Japanese society to render access exceedingly difficult, if not impossible in many cases, for foreigners.

Needless to say, objective analysis of such issues is also exceedingly difficult. Most discussion of them tends to focus on specific cases, which makes it extremely difficult to employ the usual techniques of quantification and aggregation. We look carefully at a large number of such cases in chapter 3 and make an effort to find indirect measures of the extent of Japanese protection, encompassing intangible as well as overt barriers, though without offering any promise of achieving great precision or definitively resolving the debate.

It is clear, however, whatever the economic conclusions reached here or elsewhere, that the political impact of alleged Japanese malpractices is enormous. Important elements in both industry and Congress in the United States, and their counterparts in many other parts of the world—including Japan's nearest neighbors, some of which (such as Korea and Taiwan) are also among the world's most competitive countries—believe deeply that Japan is "different" and that the difference constitutes a massive trade barrier.[12] In the United States, this view of pervasive "unfairness" has motivated many of the initiatives to retaliate against Japan. Each time a new problem is discovered for an additional product, suspicions are confirmed and the complaints grow.

As noted above, however, the extent of the problem has fluctuated quite closely with the levels of the two countries' external imbalances—both globally and bilaterally, which tend to move closely together. This brings us back to the macroeconomic and exchange rate issues, both structural and policy-related, as mentioned above. But the intensity of concerns over the sector-specific issues, and proposals for microeconomic responses to them, also rises with the aggregate imbalances.

There is a certain logic in this correlation of sector-specific and macroeconomic concerns.[13] When the aggregate positions of the countries are in rough equilibrium, fewer industries are likely to experience competitive problems—due to Japanese practices or other causes—which deny them market share. Hence, fewer will seek political redress, and the level of tension will be considerably lower.

Conversely, a rise in the macroeconomic imbalance—as manifest most directly in dollar overvaluation and yen undervaluation—adds to the problems of all industries, including the more competitive. A growing number will inevitably look for government help, with some justification as their problems derive from forces outside their own control. The nature of the help sought will almost always be sector-specific, as individual firms quite naturally focus

---

12. The European Community, in fact, brought a GATT case against Japan in 1982 which basically alleged that the very nature of its society was a nontariff barrier and that authority should be granted for retaliation against the resultant "impairment of trade concessions." The case has not been pursued, and the United States declined to join it on the ground that the charge was too general.

13. For more details see C. Fred Bergsten and John Williamson, "Exchange Rates and Trade Policy," in *Trade Policy in the 1980s,* edited by William R. Cline (Washington: Institute for International Economics, 1983).

on their own problems and remedies apparent to them. In any event, they tend to feel virtually powerless to offset broad economic forces such as exchange rates and government budgets, let alone national savings proclivities and other structural phenomena.

To the extent that evidence of ''unfair'' treatment of the petitioner's effort to compete against Japanese firms can be confirmed, his case for microeconomic responses will be buttressed. Hence the growth of macroeconomic imbalances will inevitably produce increased allegations of microeconomic distortions, adding to the escalation of tensions on both fronts. There is probably a ratchet effect of overall imbalances on sector-specific concerns: each round of sizable macroeconomic difficulties produces additions to the list of sectoral complaints, which in turn must be dealt with to return the overall relationship to anything approaching stability.

Striking a Balance

It therefore seems clear that both the macroeconomic and sector-specific issues must be addressed to deal effectively with the US-Japan economic problem that has emerged. On one hand, even an immediate elimination of all of Japan's trade barriers and distortions—both overt and intangible—would, under current macroeconomic circumstances, almost certainly leave an enormous imbalance in the external positions (global and bilateral) of the two countries. On the other hand, even a return to macroeconomic balance in the policies (especially, fiscal policies) of both would leave a long list of sector-specific complaints.

The case for attacking simultaneously the macro and micro dimensions of the problem, with all possible effort, is reinforced by three other considerations. First, we will show in chapter 2 that Japan can be expected to run substantial current account surpluses, albeit at levels much lower than at present, both globally and with the United States even under equilibrium conditions. Unlike the period just after the dollar devaluations of the early 1970s, when Japan's global surplus and bilateral surplus with the United States disappeared or dropped to very low levels, there is unlikely to be a respite from at least some substantial and continuing imbalance between the two countries.

Second, we have suggested that both the macro and micro dimensions of the problem reflect important structural elements in both countries. By definition, structural change cannot occur within brief periods of time. A substantial part of "the problem" will thus inherently take years, or even decades, to resolve even with the best of wills in both countries. The corollary is that it is essential to do everything that can possibly be done in the short run, not only to avoid the enormous economic and political costs of a systemic breakdown but also to avoid derailing the needed structural changes and thus delaying even further a lasting solution to the US-Japan problem itself.

Moreover, it is important to recognize at the outset that major structural influences may be largely beyond the governments' control, at least in the near term. Indeed, the distinction between "structure" and "policy" implies the presence of structural problems beyond the normal reach of government action. There is a dangerous potential for clash between the demands of the United States for change in the Japanese economy, on one hand, and a limited ability of the Japanese government to act in some societal areas, on the other. The analysis of chapter 3 attempts to separate the trade problems into those readily subject to action by the government of Japan, and those more inherent in the society and difficult to change.

Third, different constituencies are affected differently by changes in macroeconomic and sector-specific circumstances—and perceive the differences as even greater than they actually are. For example, exporting firms in the United States may benefit primarily from Japanese measures to liberalize specific markets, whereas import-competing firms may gain more from currency changes. More generally, beleaguered firms often fail to recognize that an exchange rate change of 20 percent can have a much more powerful impact on their competitive prospects than an alteration in testing requirements for their product. But the number of constituencies seeking sector-specific modifications has risen substantially in this latest episode of overall imbalance, as noted, and at least some significant part of them must be satisfied if the politics of the issues are to subside substantially.

From this cursory and preliminary review of the problem, we conclude that it is essential to move as quickly as possible in both the United States and Japan to address its several sets of causes: structural and policy, macro and micro. As we shall see in later chapters, however, it is the macroeconomic area that both holds the major potential for rapid improvement in the situation and has been least subject to intergovernmental negotiation to date. We shall thus stress this area throughout, particularly in our policy recommendations in chapter 4.

It is also essential to understand the limitations of the several sets of policy tools for redressing the several parts of the problem. Changes in trade *policies* are most unlikely to have a significant impact on overall trade *balances*. Improvement in the trade balances will not resolve many concerns of trade policy. Hence, there must be a much clearer matching of policy instruments to policy targets than has characterized much of the debate to date. No single device, be it a change in the dollar-yen exchange rate or a US import surcharge or a "get tough" approach to Japanese import barriers, will simultaneously redress the different aspects of the US-Japan problem. A multifaceted strategy is necessary, and will be suggested in chapter 4.

Both the history of the US-Japan economic problem and its latest manifestation highlight the enormous importance to both countries of an effectively functioning international economic system. At least to some extent, the existence of a more disciplined international monetary regime might have prevented the emergence of the recurrent dollar-yen misalignment. Better GATT mechanisms could have channeled at least some US-Japan trade conflict into orderly dispute settlement procedures. In addition to making every effort to resolve the several dimensions of their current problem, the United States and Japan thus would be well advised to make joint efforts to lead the world toward adopting more effective international economic systems as well.

The remainder of this study seeks to analyze, quantitatively and in some depth, the central issues of the problem as seen from an American perspective: the composition of the Japanese external accounts and the bilateral imbalance between the two countries; the underlying Japanese economic structure, particularly the saving-investment relationship, and its impact on the external position; the relative roles of macroeconomic influences, including the exchange rate, and sector-specific factors in generating the Japanese surpluses and their recent sharp growth; and the absolute impact of each country's trade restrictions on the other, including intangible as well as overt barriers and alleged "exchange rate manipulation" on the part of Japan. Based on these analyses, we will seek to draw more precise conclusions about the nature of the overall problem and suggest a program of policy responses to try to remedy it.

American Initiatives and Japanese Response

Before doing so, however, we will briefly review the present status of the official debate: the various US efforts to elicit policy changes in Japan, from both the administration and the Congress, and the Japanese responses.

Whatever the precise source of the current problem, congressional frustration over the large US-Japanese bilateral deficit and the widespread perception that the Japanese market is more protected than the US market—the "lack of a level playing field''—have led to a number of legislative proposals that demand liberalization by Japan under threat of retaliation. The administration has also undertaken several initiatives, aimed partly at defusing congressional pressure for more extensive action but basically seeking similar objectives. In addition, the administration is reported to have "suggested" a number of fundamental changes in the structure of the Japanese economy, and society more broadly, in an effort to address some of the deeper roots of the problem. Most recently, the United States and Japan (and Germany, the United Kingdom, and France) have launched a major program of currency intervention to attack the exchange rate imbalances directly.

In March 1985, the Senate passed by 92 to 0 a nonbinding concurrent resolution (S. Con. Res. 15) introduced by Senator John C. Danforth (R-Mo.). The resolution called for the President to restrict imports from Japan by an amount equal to the increase in US imports resulting from the relaxation of the "voluntary" restraint on automobile exports, unless Japan liberalizes its own market by an equivalent amount within 45 days. The resolution specifically cited telecommunications, electronics, and automobiles as sectors in Japan to be liberalized. It incorporated the view that reciprocity does not exist:

Whereas, Japan has extensive access to the United States market for products in which Japan has a comparative advantage;
Whereas, United States exporters lack access to the Japanese market for manufactured goods, forest products, key agricultural commodities, and certain services in which the United States has a comparative advantage; . . .[14]

Subsequently, the Senate Finance Committee passed a version of the proposal with mandatory legislative effect, going beyond a mere consensus resolution. By mid-September the bill still had not come to a vote of the full Senate, however, as action on the budget as well as other trade legislation (especially on textiles and apparel) occupied Senate attention.

For its part, the House offered a nonbinding concurrent resolution similar to the March Senate resolution.[15] Passing by a vote of 394 to 19, this

---

14. *Congressional Record,* 28 March 1985, p. S.3573.
15. House Concurrent Resolution 107.

resolution, introduced by Ways and Means Committee Chairman Dan Rostenkowski (D-Ill.), focused more attention on the macroeconomic dimension of the issue: it incorporated language urging the President to "develop a concrete plan for reducing the trade deficit by attacking its causes, including the high value of the dollar on the exchange markets."

In addition to these "reciprocity" initiatives, Senators John Heinz (R-Pa.) and Slade Gorton (R-Wash.) introduced legislation that would impose a surcharge on all imports from Japan.[16] Senator Lloyd Bentsen (D-Tex.), Congressman Richard A. Gephardt (D-Mo.), and Congressman Rostenkowski introduced the Trade Emergency and Export Promotion Act in July, which would inter alia require the administration to initiate action against major US trading partners (notably Japan) to obtain compensation for trade practices which "nullify and impair [their] obligations under the GATT"; mandate an import surcharge of 25 percent against "Japan and certain other large trading countries with excessive trade surpluses"; and, recognizing the exchange rate component of the problem, "require the Department of the Treasury to come up with a global plan to prevent fluctuations in our currency values, . . . the single most important influence on our competitiveness. . . ."[17]

Meanwhile, since the Reagan-Nakasone summit of January 1985, the administration has focused its attention on the Market-Oriented Sector-Specific (MOSS) talks. The objective has been to open the Japanese market in four key sectors where the United States should be able to exploit its comparative advantage: telecommunications, electronics, pharmaceuticals and medical equipment, and forest products. The telecommunications negotiation was keyed to the privatization of Nippon Telephone and Telegraph (NTT), which took effect on May 1, and the American negotiators have indicated that their proposals were largely accepted.[18] Efforts in the other three sectors continue, however, and have not been successfully resolved.

In June 1985, the US government reportedly conveyed a series of "suggestions" to the government of Japan concerning some of the more deeply rooted structural aspects of the trade problem. As reported in the Japanese press (and, to a limited extent, in the American press), the United

---

16. S.770 and S.906, respectively.

17. *Congressional Record,* (17 July 1985), pp. S.9630–37.

18. Lionel H. Olmer, then Under Secretary of Commerce for International Trade, and Mike Mansfield, US Ambassador to Japan, indicated in April that Japan had agreed to virtually all the changes proposed by US negotiators. *Washington Post,* 6 April and 26 April 1985. However, as noted below, US negotiators subsequently demanded further action in telecommunications.

States proposed that Japan "counter such 'invisible' barriers as the distribution system, controls and the life styles that are deeply rooted in Japanese society." Ranging over "dozens of sections," the "long recommendations" present a "structural reform plan for Japanese society."[19] The specifics reportedly call for:

• Japanese formulation of a clear import strategy to the year 2000 with specific procurement goals

• formulation of plans for structural adjustment of depressed industries in Japan

• creation of three new financial institutions to channel postal savings capital into low-interest housing loans, consumer and import financing

• tax reforms to encourage consumer spending for leisure and discourage savings

• reduction of weekly working hours

• creation of plans to speed up the restructuring of basic industries (such as textiles, wood products, and chemicals)

• amendment of present laws that protect "Mom and Pop" retail stores, thereby facilitating American-style supermarket operations.

In the face of US pressure on these several fronts, the government of Japan has responded with a market-opening package, announced on April 9, 1985, and followed by a detailed Action Program in July. In his address Prime Minister Yasuhiro Nakasone cited measures resulting from US-Japanese negotiations in the sectors cited above (telecommunications, electronics, pharmaceuticals and medical equipment, and forest products). He noted privatization of NTT, simplification of technical standards for terminal equipment, and inclusion of foreign-affiliated firms in the standards-setting council. He cited legislation to protect patent rights in semiconductor chips, amendment of the copyright law to protect computer program rights, and mutual elimination of semiconductor tariffs by Japan and the United States. He indicated that foreign clinical test data would be accepted for medical

---

19. *Asahi Shimbun*, 30 June 1985. There was a follow-up in the *Asahi Shimbun* on 7 July 1985 and a US summary by Hobart Rowen, "Japan Urged to Restructure Economy," *Washington Post*, 13 July 1985, p. A20.

equipment and pharmaceuticals, and that approval and licensing would be facilitated in these products. He stated the government's intention to "positively consider" reducing tariffs on plywood and other wood products within three years.[20]

Nakasone adopted the principle recommended by the Advisory Committee for External Economic Issues (Okita Committee) of "freedom in principle, restrictions as exceptions" with exceptions limited to a "necessary minimum."[21] He pledged further tariff reductions[22]—which have subsequently been announced, amounting to 20 percent cuts on a wide range of items and total elimination on some—and improvement in standards, certification, and import-testing procedures to encourage manufactured imports. He indicated the government's intention to attain economic growth by expansion of domestic demand. And the Prime Minister made an unprecedented appeal to the nation "to be willingly receptive toward foreign products."[23]

Subsequently, the Japanese government announced an emergency program to raise imports by $3 billion. The program was to include special credit lines at the Export–Import Bank of Japan for private sector imports; purchase of cobalt, nickel, and other metals for stockpiling; and the purchase of US grains for stockpiling in Japan and famine relief abroad. The emergency program sought to achieve immediate results, in light of the fact that the more general market-opening package would be spread over three years.[24] However, by late September it remained unclear how much of this emergency program would be implemented, and when.

On July 30, Prime Minister Nakasone announced his three-year Action Program on trade.[25] In addition to the tariff cuts previously announced, the package included reform of 88 regulations criticized by foreign businessmen. The tariff on plywood (of special concern to US negotiators) will be cut beginning in 1987. In standards and certification, there will be increased self-certification, acceptance of foreign test data, transparency through foreign participation in committees drafting standards, new time limits on processing

---

20. Statement of Prime Minister Nakasone on External Economic Measures, Tokyo, 9 April 1985.

21. Report of the Advisory Committee for External Economic Issues, Tokyo, 9 April 1985.

22. *Washington Post,* 26 June 1985.

23. *Ibid.*

24. *Journal of Commerce,* 20 June 1985.

25. Government-Ruling Parties, Joint Headquarters for the Promotion of External Economic Measures, *The Outline of the Action Program for Improved Market Access* (Tokyo, 30 July 1985; processed).

of certification, and expansion of categories not requiring import notification.[26] In government procurement, 16 entities will be added to coverage under the GATT code; competition will be expanded through reduction of single tendering, extension of bid periods, and provision of information.

The reaction to the July 30 announcement by leading congressmen was skeptical.[27] US business leaders welcomed the measures but indicated that it would take time to evaluate their effectiveness.[28] The new US Trade Representative, Clayton Yeutter, expressed disappointment that some issues were not addressed, including government procurement of telecommunications equipment and restrictions on forest and citrus products. Yeutter also regretted that many of the policy changes would not take place until 1987 or 1988.[29] Subsequently, the Reagan administration informed Japanese negotiators that, although it appreciated the July 30 package, it was necessary that Japan take immediate steps to make major import purchases and "visibly" decrease its trade surplus with the United States.[30]

Broadly, the new liberalization package appeared to have had little effect in reversing frustration with perceived Japanese trade practices, particularly in the Congress. Areas of contention clearly remained in the MOSS sectors, especially forest products. And by mid-year, US semiconductor producers sought government retaliatory action (under section 301 of the 1974 Trade Act) against Japanese producers for pursuing alleged cartel behavior that excludes imports of chips into Japan while engaging in price wars in the US market.[31] Overall, pressure for retaliatory measures against Japan remained high despite the market-opening initiatives announced by Nakasone.

In early September 1985, the Reagan administration took the next step by including Japanese cigarettes and leather goods (including footwear) on a list of items on which it would be initiating investigations under the unfair trade

---

26. In cosmetics, comprehensive licensing will replace individual licensing through lists of permissible and prohibited ingredients, cutting licenses (currently 84,000 per year) by 60 percent in three years. One-fourth of medical equipment approval procedures will be eliminated. In automobiles, cars with sales below 1,000 vehicles per year will be released for sale immediately upon arrival through acceptance of manufacturers' test data. (The government considers the existing "Type Designation System" adequate for large volume imports.) *Ibid.*
27. *Washington Post,* 31 July 1985.
28. *Journal of Commerce,* 31 July 1985.
29. *Washington Post,* 2 August 1985.
30. *Journal of Commerce,* 13 August 1985.
31. *Japan Economic Survey,* 14 June 1985, pp. 1–2; *New York Times,* 5 June 1985; *Wall Street Journal,* 14 June 1985.

provisions of US law (section 301 of the Trade Act of 1974).[32] This action was broadly interpreted as an attempt to preempt protectionist legislation in Congress. The Japanese cases in themselves would appear to hold little promise for defusing tension, however, because they, too, fail to deal significantly with the trade imbalances. Even the administration's estimates of possible increases in cigarette exports would appear to be seriously overstated (chapter 3). Moreover, it is unlikely that Japan will reverse its long practice of protecting the people who are in the socially outcast class that works in leather goods[33] or that US exports of leather products (an area of severe weakness in US competitiveness) would rise much if Japan did liberalize—although it would be desirable to bring Japan's restrictions in this area into compatibility with the GATT, perhaps by converting them into tariffs and paying due compensation to foreign suppliers.

By the autumn of 1985, there thus appeared to be a high risk of a much larger eruption of protective legislation, possibly with sufficient support to override a presidential veto. Although the pressure for trade action extended well beyond Japan, there was little doubt that the massive US-Japanese bilateral trade imbalance was the vortex of this protectionist whirlpool.

Despite all this activity on the trade question, however, very little action in either country was being addressed to the macroeconomic causes of the overall imbalances. There were extensive discussions and policy initiatives aimed at specific problems and "unfair practices." As noted above, there was also at least some discussion of the structural underpinnings of the two countries' economies. But economic policy was the missing dimension of the debate, despite its great importance.

The exchange rate initiative launched by the United States and Japan (and the rest of the Group of Five) on September 22, and followed up by President Ronald Reagan in his trade policy speech of September 23, was thus a significant new element in the equation. For the first time, the US government and its chief allies recognized publicly that the overvalued dollar was a major source of the trade problem, and resolved to act jointly to deal with it. Initial results were promising: the yen-dollar rate strengthened from 239:1 on

---

32. The other items were computers in Brazil, insurance in South Korea, and canned fruit in the EEC. *Wall Street Journal,* 9 September 1985.

33. Chalmers Johnson, *MITI and the Japanese Miracle: The Growth of Industrial Policy, 1925–1975* (Stanford, Calif.: Stanford University Press, 1982), p. 302; Ezra Vogel, *Comeback Case by Case: Building the Resurgence of American Business* (New York: Simon and Schuster, 1985), p. 98.

September 20 to 217:1 on September 27, a move of almost 10 percent in one week, as the Bank of Japan spent over a billion dollars to promote the needed correction.

Even with this rapid change, however, the trade-weighted dollar was only modestly below its 1984 average. In addition, as with previous intervention efforts, it remained unclear to what extent lasting adjustments could be achieved through this technique alone. On one hand, the United States and Japan would clearly have to maintain their new aggressiveness in the currency markets for some time to withstand the inevitable testing of their will to succeed. On the other hand, and more fundamentally, sustainable adjustment still required resolution of the fundamental problems relating to saving-investment balances and fiscal policy problems in both countries. We therefore turn now to a detailed examination of those issues in an effort to understand them better and provide a basis for policy proposals to deal with them effectively.

2 Macroeconomic Influences

One implicit premise of the recent escalation of demands for retaliation against Japan (chapter 1) is that the large US bilateral deficit with that country is attributable in considerable degree to unfair trade by Japan, primarily in the form of overt and (especially) intangible protection of its domestic market. Yet the macroeconomic forces outlined above surely have played the major role in the growing imbalance between the two countries.

The analysis of this chapter seeks to quantify the impact of macroeconomic imbalances on the bilateral trade relationship in recent years. The initial section examines US trade with all of its major trading partners to determine whether the American trade problem is uniquely with Japan, or more generalized. The discussion then considers the role of growing imbalances between domestic saving and domestic resource use for investment and fiscal deficits, in an effort to address the underlying sources of the macroeconomic problem. Estimates are then presented of the structural trade deficit that the United States could normally expect to run with Japan as a result of the triangular nature of its trade. Quantitative estimates of the impact of dollar overvaluation and economic growth on the bilateral balance conclude this chapter.

It is important to recognize at the outset that a focus on the bilateral US-Japan trade deficit is necessitated by political-economic reality. Traditional economic analysis would tend to dismiss consideration of any particular bilateral relationship and concentrate instead on the global US and Japanese balance of payments positions. The periodic intensifications of trade conflict between the United States and Japan, however, place a political-economic significance on the bilateral trade balance that it generally would not have on economic grounds alone. Moreover, in the case of the US-Japan relationship, changes in the bilateral imbalance tend to mirror changes in the global imbalance fairly accurately. The hypothesis underlying this focus of attention is that, given the history of the issue as traced in chapter 1 and

21

TABLE 2.1   **Trade balances for 25 major trading nations, total and with United States, 1980–81 to 1984**

Country	Bilateral US[a] 1984 level			
	Million dollars	Rank	Percentage of bilateral turnover	Rank
Argentina	141	20	7.3	18
Australia	−908	22	−10.5	22
Austria	365	18	33.9	9
Belgium	−2,014	23	−23.5	23
Brazil	5,633	7	51.6	3
Canada	20,387	2	18.0	14
Denmark	913	14	43.0	6
France	2,479	11	17.0	15
Germany	8,726	4	32.4	10
Hong Kong	5,837	6	48.8	4
Italy	4,129	8	32.1	11
Japan	36,795	1	43.8	5
Korea	4,044	9	25.3	12
Mexico	6,275	5	20.7	13
Norway	1,145	13	40.0	7
Netherlands	−3,224	24	−27.1	24
China, P.R.	337	19	5.9	19
Romania	720	15	59.1	1
Singapore	446	17	5.7	20
Spain	66	21	1.3	21
Sweden	1,805	12	37.9	8
Switzerland	636	16	11.0	16
Taiwan	11,065	3	52.2	2
United Kingdom	2,834	10	10.4	17
Subtotal	108,632	n.a.	n.a.	n.a.
United States	−123,209	25	−22.1	25

n.a. Not applicable.

Source: Calculations from IMF, *International Financial Statistics,* various issues; IMF, *Direction of Trade Statistics Yearbook 1984;* US Department of Commerce, *Highlights of US Export and Import Trade,* December 1981 and December 1984.

	Change, 1980–81 to 1984			Total nonoil,[b] change, 1980–81 to 1984	
Million dollars	Rank	Percentage of bilateral turnover[c]	Rank	Percentage of total country turnover[d]	Rank
1,549	17	48.5	2	38.8	2
1,015	20	15.5	19	−3.1	22
446	23	41.2	6	3.0	15
1,991	15	24.1	15	1.9	16
5,282	6	47.5	3	32.5	3
13,453	2	9.5	22	0.8	20
955	21	45.5	4	1.0	19
4,048	8	28.9	12	1.1	18
7,257	5	26.0	13	1.4	17
3,105	12	14.9	20	6.2	10
4,446	7	35.1	9	12.2	6
21,664	1	17.6	18	5.1	11
3,991	9	24.7	14	5.0	12
9,319	3	30.9	11	39.7	1
−625	24	−10.2	24	6.8	9
3,131	11	31.1	10	3.4	14
2,443	13	44.9	5	7.3	8
857	22	71.7	1	15.4	4
1,374	18	23.9	16	−6.2	24
2,009	14	40.5	7	12.5	5
1,941	16	39.5	8	4.1	13
1,352	19	22.8	17	0.8	21
7,391	4	4.7	23	11.9	7
3,607	10	13.6	21	−5.0	23
102,003	n.a.	n.a.	n.a.	n.a.	n.a.
−85,395	25	−14.4	25	−22.6	25

a. Country exports are from US data on imports, c.i.f.; country imports are from US data on exports, f.o.b. Includes oil.
b. Based on country's own data on exports, f.o.b., and imports, c.i.f.
c. 1984 ratio of bilateral balance to bilateral turnover *minus* average ratio for 1980 and 1981.
d. Nonoil.

pervasive distrust of the fairness of Japan's trading practices, pressures for retaliatory US action rise as the bilateral deficit increases.[1]

An International Perspective

Despite the political salience of the bilateral trade deficit with Japan ($36.8 billion in 1984),[2] most other countries have also improved their trade balances with the United States and globally in recent years. Table 2.1 presents data placing Japan's trade performance in the context of that recorded by the 25 largest exporting countries.

The table indicates that Japan's bilateral surplus with the United States is indeed the largest in absolute terms. However, the bilateral trade surpluses of Canada and Taiwan with the United States are also large in absolute terms ($20 billion and $11 billion, respectively). Moreover, relative to the size of each country's bilateral trade turnover (imports plus exports) with the United States, four other major trading nations (Romania, Taiwan, Brazil, and Hong Kong) have larger surpluses with the United States than Japan.

The contribution of each country to the change in the US trade balance from the average of 1980–81 to 1984 is also shown in table 2.1. On this criterion, Japan again ranks highest in absolute terms, with Canada ranking a closer second than before, followed by Mexico and Taiwan. However, when the change in bilateral trade balance is stated relative to each country's bilateral trade turnover with the United States in 1980–81 and in 1984,[3] 17 of the 24 countries examined have had larger relative increases than Japan. The median increase in bilateral surplus with the United States was 28.9 percent of bilateral trade turnover, while the increase for Japan was 17.6 percent.

---

1. Because Japan is so widely believed to be practicing unfair trade, this hypothesis is consistent with the absence of corresponding pressure for US retaliation against Canada and other countries that also have proportionately large and growing trade surpluses with the United States (as indicated below) but do not have the same "unfair" image as Japan.

2. Exports f.o.b. (free on board) minus imports c.i.f. (cost including insurance and freight). Note that trade balance figures differ depending on whether imports are stated c.i.f. or f.o.b. The bilateral trade data recorded by the two countries can also differ somewhat (because of differing times for registering transactions, for example).

3. That is, $z_1 - z_0$, where $z = (X - M)/(X + M)$, X = exports, M = imports, and subscripts 0 and 1 refer to 1980–81 and 1984, respectively.

A similar conclusion is reached if a still broader perspective is adopted. Considering global trade balances rather than bilateral balances with the United States, and referring to nonoil trade,[4] Japan stands approximately in the middle of the field of the large trading nations in terms of relative increases in trade surpluses. Japan's total nonoil trade balance relative to its nonoil trade turnover rose by 5.1 percentage points from 1980–81 (when this ratio was 25.3 percent) to 1984 (30.3 percent), placing Japan eleventh out of 25 countries (with the United States last by a wide margin).

These comparisons suggest that Japan's high visibility in US political concern over the trade deficit stems primarily from the large scale of Japan's trade, as well as the public image of Japan as unfair in its trading practices, rather than from any exceptional percentage rise in its bilateral surplus with the United States or globally, relative to Japan's trade base. Moreover, the evidence presented here shows that Japan is only one of many major trading nations with similar trends in trade with the United States. This pattern would suggest that the problem of large US trade deficits is far broader than a bilateral US-Japan problem. Indeed, the most striking figure in table 2.1 is that, while the median country has increased its global nonoil trade balance from 1980–81 to 1984 by 5 percent of turnover, the US balance has declined by 22.6 percent. Indeed, the only two other countries showing declines have experienced far smaller reductions (6 percent). This pattern suggests that the improving trade balances of most major trading countries (excluding the Organization of Petroleum Exporting Countries, OPEC) from 1980 to 1984 were primarily the mirror image of a soaring US trade deficit.

The Saving-Investment Imbalance

An important factor in the macroeconomic environment underlying the growing US-Japanese external imbalances in recent years has been the rising divergence in the two countries' respective balances between domestic saving and investment. This balance has been declining for the United States and rising for Japan. Because the difference between domestic saving and

---

4. Oil trade is excluded because its substantial dollar-price erosion from 1980 to 1984 distorts trends in real trade. In any event, the decline in oil imports from 1980 to 1984 was approximately 5 percent of total 1984 imports for both Japan and the United States. IMF, *International Financial Statistics*, July 1985, pp. 278, 486.

TABLE 2.2   **Saving, investment, and external current account as percentage of GNP, 1970–84**

	Private saving			Private investment (D)
	Personal (A)	Business (B)	Total (C)	
United States				
1970	5.6	10.4	16.0	14.5
1971	5.6	11.1	16.7	15.4
1972	4.4	11.5	16.0	16.4
1973	6.0	11.2	17.2	17.3
1974	5.9	10.4	16.4	15.9
1975	6.1	12.2	18.2	13.3
1976	4.8	12.3	17.1	15.0
1977	4.1	13.0	17.0	16.9
1978	4.1	13.2	17.3	17.9
1979	4.0	12.8	16.8	17.5
1980	4.2	12.4	16.5	15.3
1981	4.6	12.6	17.2	16.4
1982	4.4	12.6	17.1	13.5
1983	3.6	13.7	17.3	14.3
1984	4.3	14.2	18.4	17.4
Japan[a]				
1970	11.5	22.0	33.1	33.9
1971	11.6	21.0	30.8	29.5
1972	11.9	20.4	31.9	29.6
1973	14.0	18.4	32.0	32.6
1974	16.8	13.3	29.7	31.1
1975	16.1	13.0	28.6	26.0
1976	16.5	14.2	30.2	25.9
1977	15.2	14.5	29.2	23.8
1978	14.7	16.2	30.3	23.1
1979	13.2	16.0	28.6	24.8
1980	13.8	15.5	28.7	25.2
1981	14.0	14.9	28.2	23.8
1982	12.5	15.4	27.3	23.0
1983	12.8	15.2	26.4	21.1
1984	12.5	15.9	26.1	20.9

Source: Council of Economic Advisers, *Economic Report of the President 1985*, pp. 232, 262, 321; *Federal Reserve Bulletin*, May 1985, p. A53; IMF, *International Financial Statistics Yearbook 1984*, pp. 363–65, 595; OECD, *Quarterly National Accounts*, vol. 2, 1984, pp. 36–39; and OECD staff.

| Government balance | | Saving-investment balance | Current account |
Structural (E)	Actual (F)	$(G = C - D + F)$	(H)
−1.5	−1.1	0.4	0.2
−2.1	−1.8	−0.5	−0.1
−2.0	−0.3	−0.7	−0.5
−1.5	0.6	0.5	0.5
−0.6	−0.3	0.2	0.1
−2.4	−4.1	0.8	1.2
−1.8	−2.1	0.0	0.2
−2.0	−0.9	−0.8	−0.8
−1.6	0.0	−0.6	−0.7
−0.9	0.6	−0.1	0.0
−1.4	−1.2	0.0	0.0
−0.9	−0.9	−0.1	0.2
−1.9	−3.8	−0.2	−0.3
−2.7	−4.1	−1.1	−1.3
−3.4	−3.4	−2.4	−2.8
1.9	1.8	1.0	1.0
1.7	1.2	2.5	2.5
0.6	−0.1	2.2	2.2
0.3	0.6	0.0	0.0
0.7	0.4	−1.0	−1.0
−1.9	−2.7	−0.1	−0.1
−2.9	−3.7	0.7	0.7
−3.1	−3.8	1.6	1.6
−4.9	−5.5	1.7	1.8
−4.3	−4.8	−0.9	−0.9
−4.1	−4.5	−1.0	−1.0
−3.5	−4.0	0.4	0.4
−2.8	−3.6	0.6	0.6
−2.2	−3.5	1.8	1.8
−1.3	−2.6	2.6	2.6

a. Sum of gross business saving and household saving exceeds private saving because of statistical discrepancy.

investment determines the size of the country's external current account surplus or deficit, and because this global external balance then affects the bilateral trade balance (as analyzed below), structural trends in saving and investment play an important role in the bilateral trade relationship.

From national accounts identities, the excess of domestic investment over domestic private and government saving *equals* the country's current account deficit and its net inflow of capital from abroad (foreign saving).[5] Table 2.2 presents the balance of saving and investment for the United States and Japan for 1970–84. Total private saving *less* private investment *plus* (or *minus)* the government's fiscal balance (surplus or deficit, including state and local) *equals* the total saving-investment balance. The final column reports the external current account balance. All data are expressed as percentages of GNP. Except for statistical discrepancy, the difference between domestic saving (including fiscal balance) and investment should equal the current account balance.

The table immediately highlights the atypical nature of the recent US external deficit. From 1970 to 1982, the average US current account balance was zero. But in 1983, the current account fell to a deficit of 1.3 percent of GNP, and in 1984 the deficit widened to 2.8 percent of GNP. For Japan, the divergence from long-term averages has been in the opposite direction. From 1970 through 1982, the global current account averaged a surplus of only 0.6 percent of GNP—a smaller figure than normally associated with the image of Japan as a surplus country—but in 1983 the surplus reached 1.8 percent, and in 1984 it was 2.6 percent of GNP. The rising bilateral imbalance between the two countries has paralleled this divergent trend toward sharply higher current account deficits in the United States and current account surpluses in Japan.

The table indicates the sharp difference between the level of private saving in Japan and the United States. Gross private saving (not deducting capital consumption allowance) has been in the range of 30 percent of GNP in Japan, compared with approximately 17 percent of GNP in the United States.

---

5. From the product side of national accounts, $Y = C + I + G + X - M$, where Y is GNP, C is consumption, I is investment, G is government spending, X is exports of goods and services, and M is imports of goods and services. From the income side of national accounts, $Y = C + S + T$, where S is saving and T is taxes. Subtracting and rearranging, $S - I - (G - T) = X - M$. The gap between resources available from saving and resources used in investment and government deficit (left-hand side) must be filled by net resources from abroad (right-hand side).

The largest difference has been in household saving, which for Japan has been nearly three times as high (14 percent of GNP) as in the United States (4 percent to 5 percent). Gross business saving shows a much smaller difference (averaging approximately 17 percent of GNP in Japan and 12 percent in the United States).

Japan's traditionally high level of personal saving may reflect such institutional influences as the previously low level of social security benefits, a wage system with large lump-sum bonuses twice a year, exemption from taxes on interest earned from savings, and the limited availability of consumer and housing credit.[6] The relatively low level of US personal saving, despite periodic tax incentives to saving, has been a feature of American society for many decades, and the level has declined still further in the last decade (table 2.2).

Recent trends especially have been affected by the long-term decline in the rate of private investment in Japan, from an average of 26 percent of GNP in 1970–74 to 24.8 percent in 1975–80 and 22.2 percent in 1981–84. Declining investment appears to have been associated primarily with the deceleration in Japan's growth rate, with a resulting reduction in domestic market prospects for new investment.

With private saving relatively constant or declining only modestly, and private investment declining more sharply, Japan had a growing potential surplus in its saving-investment balance. In the period 1975–81, this potential rise was more than absorbed by the rise in government deficits to a new and relatively high plateau (averaging 4.1 percent of GNP, compared to an average *surplus* of 1.0 percent in 1970–74). However, by 1982–83 and especially 1984, reductions in the fiscal deficit took place even as the domestic investment rate fell still further, instead of rising to compensate for lower fiscal absorption of private saving. As a result, by 1984 Japan had an excess of domestic saving over investment and net government borrowing amounting to 2.6 percent of GNP. As shown in the data on the ''structural'' government deficit, this trend reflected conscious government policy of tightening the fiscal balance. Thus, from 1978 to 1984, fiscal policy as measured by the

---

6. Henry C. Wallich and Mable I. Wallich, ''Banking and Finance,'' in *Asia's New Giant: How the Japanese Economy Works,* edited by Hugh Patrick and Henry Rosovsky (Washington: Brookings Institution, 1976), pp. 256–61; and Chalmers Johnson, *MITI and the Japanese Miracle: The Growth of Industrial Policy, 1925–1975* (Stanford, Calif.: Stanford University Press, 1982), p. 14.

structural (high employment) budget deficit tightened from −4.9 percent of GNP to −1.3 percent.

Even as Japan's fiscal deficits were declining and leaving a rising surplus of savings over domestic financial absorption, the opposite was happening in the United States. There the consolidated fiscal balance of the federal, state, and local governments shifted from a surplus of 0.6 percent of GNP in 1979 to a deficit averaging 3.8 percent in 1982–84. Although the actual deficit in 1982 was aggravated by recession (which caused the deficit to double from its structural, high-employment level), by 1984 the fiscal deficit reflected government policy rather than cyclical weakness (and the structural deficit reached 3.4 percent of GNP, compared to an average of 1.6 percent in 1970–82).

While the loosening of fiscal policy clearly contributed to the deteriorating saving-investment balance for the United States, the role of rising investment is less clear. Table 2.2 shows a rise in the rate of private investment from 15.3 percent of GNP in 1980 to 17.4 percent in 1984. Economic recovery and favorable changes in the tax treatment of depreciation stimulated investment. Nonetheless, the 1980 base was depressed by recession, and the 1984 level was no higher than in 1977–79. The popular image of a US investment bonanza that has siphoned off capital from the rest of the world is probably exaggerated. The depressive effect of high interest rates on many forms of investment, including construction, appears to have offset substantially the stimulative effect of tax incentives for investment in plant and equipment. It is more a fiscal bust than an investment boom that has commandeered foreign capital for domestic use in the United States.

Declining private investment and tightening fiscal policy in Japan, combined with loosening fiscal policy in the United States, drove a growing wedge between their respective saving-investment balances that meant a corresponding increase in the differences between their external balances. Japan's financial balance (private saving *plus* fiscal balance *minus* private investment) shifted from −1.0 percent of GNP in 1980 to 2.6 percent in 1984, a shift of 3.6 percentage points, as its fiscal deficit declined from 4.5 percent of GNP to 2.6 percent (a change of 1.9 percentage points, with an even larger decline in the structural deficit) and its investment fell from 25.2 percent of GNP to 20.9 percent (4.3 percentage points). The US financial balance shifted from zero in 1980 to −2.4 percent in 1984, as the fiscal deficit rose by 2.2 percentage points of GNP (accounting for virtually the full decline in the financial balance).

The difference between the US financial balance and that of Japan rose from + 1 percent of GNP in 1980 to − 5 percent in 1984. The same large reversal occurred (by accounting definition) in the difference between the two countries' external balances. This growing divergence was the underlying factor driving the sharp rise in the bilateral trade imbalance.

In sum, the macroeconomic trends that have created a growing shortfall of domestic saving from domestic investment and government borrowing in the United States, and a growing surplus in the same balances for Japan, have caused the growing bilateral trade imbalance between the two countries. The causal chain linking the saving-investment imbalances to the trade deficit appears to have been as follows in recent years. The financial shortfall within the United States caused by large fiscal deficits, in combination with relatively tight monetary policy, meant high interest rates that attracted foreign capital to fill the financial gap (and kept domestic capital at home). These capital inflows bid up the price of the dollar.[7] The high dollar made US goods uncompetitive and caused a growing deficit on the trade account, yielding an external current account deficit to match the internal gap between saving, on the one hand, and private investment and fiscal deficits on the other.[8]

The policy implication is that changes in the domestic saving-investment balance of the two countries must occur if the external disequilibrium and exchange rate misalignment are to be corrected on a lasting basis. This may require changes in both policy and underlying economic structures. For the United States, the key need is reduction of the fiscal deficit. Any boost to

---

7. To be sure, the fiscal deficit is not the only cause of the strong dollar and US current account deficits. Safe-haven considerations, more rapid US economic growth, and lower US inflation prospects may all have added to the strength of the dollar. The American current account deficit has been increased by the "growth gap" between the United States and other industrial countries, and by the import cutback of debt-ridden developing countries. But the major change has been in the fiscal situation, and its resolution seems the most promising course for policy response. See Stephen Marris, *Deficits and the Dollar: The World Economy at Risk,* POLICY ANALYSES IN INTERNATIONAL ECONOMICS 14 (Washington: Institute for International Economics, December 1985).

8. At some times, however, the exchange rate may drive the saving-investment balance rather than the reverse. If exchange market expectations are extrapolative of past trends, for example, an expectational "bubble" of dollar strength could occur, causing a large external deficit. Under these circumstances, the domestic saving-investment gap would have to widen in response. Increased consumption in response to lower import prices, and lower saving resulting from lower GNP caused by lower net exports, are examples of how the saving-investment gap might adjust to a larger external deficit. There may well have been an element of this effect in the dollar run-up of 1980–85, particularly in its latter stages.

domestic saving would also help, but saving has been relatively insensitive to policy measures in the past. For Japan, the implication is that increased domestic investment, some reversal in the reduction of fiscal deficits, some moderation in the saving rate, or some combination of all three, is necessary for a return toward financial and external balance.

Consideration of the saving-investment balance also suggests that structural tendencies in both countries could leave them with a large bilateral trade deficit for a long time, even after some correction of policies, though presumably a deficit that would be considerably smaller in relative terms than is being experienced now. Even after some rebound of investment in Japan, excess saving could continue to be a feature of the Japanese economy, as noted above. Indeed, as a mature creditor nation, Japan would normally be expected to supply net savings to the rest of the world. For its part, the United States is likely to run sizable fiscal deficits in the future even if budget action significantly reduces their relative size.

For these reasons, a long-term structural deficit of some magnitude could persist in the global current account of the United States and a long-term surplus could persist in the global current account of Japan. As analyzed below, a Japanese global surplus would almost surely mean a bilateral surplus with the United States, and this bilateral imbalance would be increased by a global US current account deficit. In short, ongoing bilateral imbalance of some substantial magnitude may be expected as a consequence of structural features of the two economies.

Other Structural Influences on the Bilateral Balance

Japan's tendency toward an excess of savings over domestic resource use tends to lead to an underlying trade surplus, globally and with the United States in particular, even when other influences such as the exchange rate and the cyclical status of both economies are neutral. But, even in the absence of a surplus of savings over domestic resource use, Japan would tend to run a trade surplus with the United States because of the phenomenon of triangular trade. In addition, Japan's overall merchandise trade has tended to be in surplus in the past to pay for its previous deficit on services and transfers. This section accepts the proposition that some Japanese structural current account surplus will tend to exist, and then seeks to determine the implications for the global and bilateral trade balances as a consequence of alternative hypothesized levels of the current account surplus.

The most obvious structural source of a trade surplus for Japan in the past has been the country's chronic deficit on services. Table 2.3 presents Japan's trade, current account, and services balances for 1977–84. The deficit on services and transfers reached $15 billion in 1981, and meant a need for offsetting surpluses on trade just to achieve a current account balance.

Approximately one-fifth of Japan's total trade turnover is with the United States. Thus, in the absence of other factors, the US share in Japan's trade surplus needed to offset Japan's historical deficit on services might have amounted to approximately $2 billion to $3 billion in recent years. This source of the bilateral deficit was always relatively limited, however. Moreover, it is likely to disappear altogether in the near future because the rapid rise in Japan's external assets means that Japan is rapidly becoming the largest creditor country in the world—so that its services account will soon reach balance and even turn into surplus, as the result of large earnings on its net investment position abroad.

For its part, triangular trade means that bilateral trade between two countries need not be balanced for the global trade of each to be in balance. Japan relies heavily on imports of oil and raw materials, primarily from OPEC and the developing countries (and Australia). Japan exports manufactured products, with a considerable portion directed to the US market. The United States exports agricultural and manufactured goods, with heavy reliance on European and developing-country markets.

This triangle of trade means that the bilateral balance of the United States with Japan tends to be in deficit, while the US balance with Europe and the developing countries is generally in surplus.[9] Moreover, the US deficit with OPEC is smaller in relative terms than Japan's, because of domestic availability of oil and other energy resources in the United States. Thus, in 1980 the United States had a bilateral deficit of $12 billion with Japan (and a deficit

---

9. Noting that the bulk of Japan's imports are "raw or lightly processed materials" and that the United States itself is an importer of many types of raw materials, Peter A. Petri finds it "natural that US exports play a modest role in Japanese imports." By applying each country's shares in world trade (detailed by 12 product classes) to the product composition and level of the other country's imports, and after taking account of the fact that each country's share in the other's imports is about twice its share in world trade, Petri is able to predict almost exactly the total levels of bilateral US-Japan trade (and the sizable bilateral deficit) in 1980 from the composition of total imports in each country. Peter A. Petri, *Modeling Japanese–American Trade: A Study of Asymmetric Interdependence* (Cambridge, Mass.: Harvard University Press, 1984), pp. 96–97.

TABLE 2.3   **Japan's trade and current account balances, 1977–84 (billion dollars)**

	1977	1978	1979
Exports, f.o.b.	81.08	98.35	102.30
To United States	20.08	25.36	26.45
Imports, f.o.b.	64.42	71.74	100.12
From United States	11.28	13.47	18.38
Trade balance, f.o.b.	16.66	26.61	2.18
With United States	8.80	11.89	8.07
Current account balance	10.88	17.53	− 8.71
Balance on services and transfers	− 5.78	− 9.08	− 10.89
Percentage of turnover	− 3.97	− 5.34	− 5.38

Source: IMF, *Balance of Payments Statistics,* vol. 3b, no. 1, January 1985; IMF, *World Economic Outlook,* April 1985, p. 236; IMF, *International Financial Statistics,* various issues; IMF, *Direction of Trade Statistics Yearbook 1984.*

of nearly $7 billion with Canada), but US trade showed a large surplus with Europe, Australia, and New Zealand ($18 billion), and a significant surplus with nonoil developing countries ($5 billion). And although the US deficit with oil-exporting countries was large ($40 billion), it was much smaller in relative terms than Japan's deficit with these countries (at 8.4 percent of trade turnover for the United States, compared with 14.6 percent for Japan).[10]

It is possible to obtain approximate estimates of the structural bilateral deficit attributable to triangular trade. Table 2.4 shows the geographical distribution of Japan's trade. The table indicates that the United States and the nonoil developing countries as a group are each comparable in size as trading partners for Japan, with each area generating annual bilateral trade surpluses for Japan in the range of $10 billion to $15 billion in the early 1980s. Other industrial countries form a group that is somewhat smaller as a trading partner for Japan, and Japan's bilateral surplus with this group is about half the size of its surplus with the United States and the nonoil developing countries. Finally, the oil-exporting countries are a fourth group that is comparable in trade magnitude to the first two (turnover of $60 billion

10. IMF, *Direction of Trade Statistics Yearbook 1984,* pp. 228, 385.

1980	1981	1982	1983	1984
130.44	151.50	138.40	146.96	169.70
31.91	38.88	36.55	43.34	60.43
129.34	130.89	120.30	115.94	124.90
22.53	23.18	22.18	22.74	24.67
1.10	20.61	18.10	31.02	44.80
9.38	15.70	14.37	20.60	35.76
− 10.74	5.12	6.98	20.94	36.40
− 11.84	− 15.49	− 11.12	− 10.08	− 8.40
− 4.56	− 5.49	− 4.30	− 3.83	− 2.85

to $70 billion annually), but Japan runs a large trade deficit with these countries.

Table 2.4 indicates the share of US trade in the totals for Japan. From 1977 to 1983, the average US share in Japan's imports was 18.3 percent. In contrast, the average share of US purchases in total exports from Japan was 26.1 percent. The difference between these two percentages represents the net influence of triangular trade on bilateral flows between the two countries.

Appendix A sets forth a simple model to determine bilateral US-Japanese trade balances as a function of the three structural influences examined in this section. The model incorporates the services balance and triangular trade, just discussed, as well as the influence of Japan's overall current account surplus on the bilateral US-Japan trade balance. The model assumes that the US shares in Japan's exports and imports remain at their average 1978–83 levels: respectively, 26.1 percent and 18.3 percent (table 2.4).[11] Because

---

11. These shares omit the 1984 experience because the longer term triangular trade phenomenon should not be confused with the distorting effects of dollar overvaluation. The use of 1977–1983 as the base period for the trade share parameters leaves little if any such bias, because undervaluation of the dollar in 1978–80 broadly offsets overvaluation in 1981–83.

TABLE 2.4   **Japan's trade, by region[a] (billion dollars and percentage)**

	1977	1978	1979
United States			
Exports	20.08	25.36	26.45
Imports	12.48	14.93	20.31
Trade balance	7.60	10.43	6.14
Other industrial countries			
Exports	16.15	18.82	20.25
Imports	14.22	17.20	20.97
Trade balance	1.93	1.62	−0.72
Oil-exporting countries			
Exports	11.87	14.18	13.24
Imports	25.18	25.55	37.33
Trade balance	−13.37	−11.37	−24.09
Nonoil developing countries			
Exports	25.07	31.45	33.69
Imports	16.42	18.64	26.41
Trade balance	8.65	12.81	7.28
Total[b]			
Exports	81.08	98.34	102.29
United States (percentage)	24.8	25.8	25.9
Imports	71.33	79.90	109.83
United States (percentage)	17.5	18.7	18.5
Trade balance	9.75	18.44	−7.54

Source: IMF, *Direction of Trade Statistics Yearbook 1984,* p. 228.
a. Exports, f.o.b.; imports, c.i.f.
b. Total exceeds sum of individual categories by the amount of trade with the USSR, Eastern Europe, and unspecified areas.

Japan's growing surplus on capital earnings is expected to eliminate its deficit on services and transfers, these balances are assumed to be zero, so that the trade balance equals the current account balance. Starting from the ratio of exports to GNP in 1983, the model calculates the trade flows that would result at alternative levels of current account surplus as a percentage of GNP for Japan. For these calculations, it is assumed that two-thirds of any

1980	1981	1982	1983	
31.91	38.18	36.55	43.34	
24.57	25.28	24.19	24.80	
7.34	13.60	12.36	18.54	
27.21	31.40	28.95	30.78	
22.90	24.10	22.17	22.92	
4.31	7.30	6.78	7.86	
18.58	22.93	21.97	19.41	
58.22	56.77	50.13	44.18	
− 39.64	− 33.84	− 28.16	− 24.77	
42.31	47.07	41.02	43.93	
30.85	31.75	30.55	30.16	
11.46	15.32	10.47	13.77	
130.44	151.50	138.44	147.00	
24.5	25.7	26.4	29.5	
141.28	142.87	131.57	126.52	
17.4	17.7	18.4	19.6	
− 10.84	8.63	6.87	20.48	

corresponding rise in the trade balance is achieved through increased Japanese exports and one-third through a reduction in Japanese imports (on grounds that imports are relatively noncompressible given their concentration in raw material inputs into production).

The results of this exercise appear in table 2.5. The current account and trade balances range from zero to 4 percent of GNP, or from zero to $48.9

TABLE 2.5   **Total and bilateral external accounts for Japan under alternative structural surplus assumptions**[a]

Total	Percentage of	Percentage				
		A	B	C	D	E
Current account and						
trade balance[c]	Income	0	1.0	2.0	3.0	4.0
Exports, f.o.b.	Income	11.5	12.2	12.8	13.5	14.2
Imports, c.i.f.	Income	11.5	11.2	10.8	10.5	10.2
Bilateral trade with United States						
Exports, f.o.b.	Exports	26.1[d]	26.1[d]	26.1[d]	26.1[d]	26.1[d]
Imports, c.i.f.	Imports	18.3[d]	18.3[d]	18.3[d]	18.3[d]	18.3[d]
Trade balance	Exports	7.8	9.3	10.7	11.8	13.0

Source: Authors' calculations.
a. Alternative cases A to E assume increments of 1 percentage point for current account and trade surplus as percentage of GNP.
b. Based on estimated 1984 GNP of $1,223 billion.
c. Assumes balance on services and transfers is zero.
d. Average percentage of total exports (or imports) in 1977–83.

billion. Taking account of the US share in Japan's exports and imports, the resulting bilateral trade surpluses with the United States range from a minimum of $11.0 billion to a maximum of $22.6 billion.[12]

In 1983, Japan's current account surplus was 1.81 percent of GNP. Case C in table 2.5 shows the calculated balances for a current account surplus of

---

12. Note that the trade shares applied in the model yield a less than proportionate rise in the US-Japan deficit as Japan's current account surplus rises, but a more than proportionate rise in the deficit for other areas. As the current account balance moves from zero to $48.9 billion, Japan's trade balance with other areas changes from − $11 billion to + $26.3 billion, while the balance with the United States rises only from $11.0 billion to $22.6 billion. This result occurs because of the differences in the initial positions. Japan's large deficit with OPEC leaves a deficit in non-US trade at zero current account and trade balance. But the trade balance, as a residual between imports and exports, rises sharply as Japan's exports rise. Expressed as a fraction of 1983 trade turnover, the rise in bilateral balance, as Japan's current account balance rises from zero to 4 percent of GNP, is actually somewhat smaller for other areas (12.7 percent) than for the United States (16.8 percent).

Value (billion dollars)[b]				
A	B	C	D	E
0	12.2	24.5	36.7	48.9
140.5	148.7	156.9	165.1	173.3
140.5	136.5	132.5	128.4	124.4
36.7	38.8	41.0	43.0	45.3
25.7	24.9	24.2	23.5	22.7
11.0	13.9	16.8	19.5	22.6

2 percent of GNP. In this case, the total current account (and trade) surplus is $24.5 billion, and the estimated bilateral trade surplus with the United States $16.8 billion. Of this total bilateral surplus, the three structural influences discussed in this section make the following contributions: services deficit, zero (as discussed above); current account surplus, $5.8 billion (based on the difference between the bilateral surplus in this case and in the alternative case A where the current account is at zero); and triangular trade, the remainder, or approximately $11 billion.

The actual bilateral trade balance in 1983 was $20.6 billion (table 2.3; if US data are used and US imports are valued c.i.f., the figure was $21.7 billion, table 2.7 below). The actual 1983 bilateral deficit included approximately $2 billion attributable to Japan's deficit on services in that year (assumed to be zero in the forward-looking analysis of table 2.5). Thus, almost two-thirds of the total bilateral deficit in 1983 was attributable to the structural influences of services deficit and triangular trade (a total of $13 billion). Most of the rest was associated with Japan's current account surplus.

For its part, the current account surplus depends on a complex set of factors. An overvalued dollar and undervalued yen tend to yield a larger current account surplus for Japan. So does a rise in US growth relative to Japanese growth, or an increase in the level of Japan's savings compared to its investment (or a corresponding decline in the difference between the two in the United States). The following section seeks to quantify the roles of the exchange rate and income level, and the investment-saving imbalance has been discussed above.

For purposes of the present section, the principal finding is that Japan's triangular trade predetermines a US bilateral deficit in the range of $11 billion annually. If in addition one might consider Japan's long-term current account surplus (in the absence of exchange rate misalignments) to be in the range of 1 to 1½ percent of GNP,[13] the "normal" structural bilateral imbalance between the United States and Japan lies in the range of $13.9 billion to $15.4 billion annually (table 2.5), at 1983 prices (table 2.5, case B, and average between cases B and C). Allowing for perhaps 20 percent inflation of the dollar price of US imports from Japan after correction of the overvalued dollar (estimated at 27 percent rise in the number of dollars per yen, combined with a pass-through rate of three-fourths to export prices; see discussion below), the normal structural bilateral deficit could rise to a range of $21.7 billion to $23.4 billion. Broadly, a structural bilateral deficit in the range of $20 billion to $25 billion may be expected as the consequence of triangular trade and a more normal current account surplus for Japan (after taking account of dollar-price increase from a correction of the overvalued dollar).

The conclusion that such a large bilateral deficit exists structurally is essentially independent of one's views on relative protection in Japan and the United States. If Japan reduced its protection, it would tend to export more to offset the increase in imports as long as there was no lasting change in its saving-investment balance. Trade and current account balances would be relatively unchanged. (Indeed, trade policy problems might *increase* as a result of Japan's increased penetration of foreign markets.)

The geographical pattern of trade might alter if the United States and Europe correspondingly eliminated protection against Japan, to the extent

---

13. Based on the EPA model, Yoshitomi estimates Japan's long-term high-employment surplus on current account at 1 to 1½ percent of GNP. See footnote 8, chapter 1, and also Masaru Yoshitomi, *Japan as Capital Exporter and the World Economy,* Occasional Paper No. 18 (New York: Group of Thirty, 1985), p. 9.

that one area or the other is more restrictive against Japanese goods. But it is the underlying economic factors of triangular trade and a significant "normal" excess of saving over investment in Japan, not protection, that produce the sizable base of an ongoing US deficit in trade with Japan. A significant US bilateral deficit is thus likely to exist even when both countries are in global balance.[14]

The Exchange Rate and Growth

Finally, we return to the global American and Japanese imbalances—which, as noted, go far to explain the bilateral imbalance between them. Much of this imbalance, and perhaps even the full amount of its increase in recent years, may be attributable to macroeconomic influences (rather than heightened protection by Japan). Two dominant macro forces are the exchange rate and economic growth in the United States and Japan. Both relate directly to the saving-investment balances just discussed.

If the dollar is overvalued, the result will be excessive US imports and weak exports in comparison with the situation that would exist at an exchange rate more accurately reflecting underlying competitive positions. To the extent that Japanese economic growth has been more sluggish or US growth more rapid than traditionally experienced, the result would be to boost US demand for imports and depress Japanese demand for imports from more normal levels.

As shown in table 2.6, the dollar appreciated by approximately 20 percent in real terms relative to the yen from 1980 to 1982 and then remained at this

---

14. In the very long run, all this might change very substantially. As noted in chapter 1, Japan is rapidly becoming the largest creditor country in the world and could build a net creditor position of as much as $500 billion by the early 1990s. It will thus be earning sizable income on its international investment position and it could be expected to run a merchandise trade deficit, perhaps of a sizable magnitude, even if its overall current account remained in surplus. It is also possible—though much more conjectural—that Japan's saving-investment relationship will return to savings *shortage*, not because of rapid investment growth as in the 1960s but due to the huge demands of an aging population on the government budget. Some leading Japanese economists believe that the Japanese budget deficit will reach a minimum of 8 percent of GNP by the end of the century, compared with about 3 percent now—more than offsetting the current excess savings over investment in the private sector. Unfortunately, however, any such "remedies" are too far in the future to help resolve the immediate, or even medium-term, problem caused by the US-Japan imbalance.

TABLE 2.6   **Actual and hypothetical exchange rates and growth rates,
United States and Japan, 1980–84 (index and percentage)**

	1980	1981	1982	1983	1984
Real exchange rate (index)					
Yen/dollar					
Actual	100.0	105.5	121.1	118.2	121.6
Hypothetical	100.0	100.4	100.6	101.3	96.0
Yen/other currencies					
Actual	100.0	95.7	107.2	103.1	100.6
Hypothetical	100.0	100.0	100.0	100.0	100.0
Domestic growth (percentage)					
Actual					
United States	−0.3	2.5	−2.1	3.7	6.8
Japan	4.8	4.0	3.3	3.4	5.8
Hypothetical					
Japan	n.a.	4.3	−0.3	5.5	8.6

n.a. Not applicable.
Source: See text.

higher plateau through 1984. That is, the number of real yen (deflating by the Japanese wholesale price index for manufactures) per real dollar (deflating by the US wholesale prices) rose by approximately one-fifth from 1980 to 1982. This real appreciation of the dollar encouraged US imports from Japan and discouraged exports to Japan.[15]

During the same period, US economic growth fluctuated sharply, from −2.1 percent in 1982 to 6.8 percent in 1984. Japanese growth was more stable, troughing at 3.3 percent in 1982 and rebounding to 5.8 percent in 1984. However, in the early 1980s, average growth in Japan was somewhat

---

15. The real exchange rate between the yen and other major currencies besides the dollar showed little trend in this period. Real appreciation of the yen relative to European currencies was offset by real depreciation of the yen relative to the Canadian dollar by 1982. (Canada bulks large in the US import weights applied in the index.)

lower relative to average growth in the United States than in previous years. In 1961–70, average growth in Japan was 9.1 percent, compared to 4.0 percent in the United States. In 1971–80, the corresponding averages were 5.0 percent and 3.2 percent, for an average differential of 1.8 percentage points. In 1981–84, growth in Japan averaged 4.1 percent while the US rate averaged 2.7 percent, a differential of only 1.4 percentage points and a continuation of the long-term trend toward reduction in Japanese growth relative to the rate in the United States.

The influence of these macroeconomic effects may be examined by considering the patterns of US-Japanese trade that would have occurred under more "normal" exchange rates and relative growth in the past four years. Table 2.6 indicates "hypothetical" levels of real exchange rate between the yen and the dollar, and the yen and other currencies, that would have existed in 1981–84 if the yen and dollar had been at their "fundamental equilibrium exchange rates" (FEERs). These rates are consistent with sustainable long-term current and capital account positions, encompassing a small level of net capital inflows for the United States rather than the large inflows of recent years.[16] As indicated in the table, correction of the rate to its FEER by 1984 would have meant an appreciation of approximately 27 percent in the yen (21 percent decline in the dollar). At mid-1985, the correction would have been even greater.[17]

Similarly, table 2.6 shows the hypothetical growth rates for Japan that would have occurred if the average 1970s differential of 1.8 percentage points above US growth had been maintained. Although this hypothetical rate is lower than the actual rate in 1982, it is higher otherwise.

Table 2.7 presents data on US-Japanese trade since 1980, as well as estimates of trade that could have occurred under different exchange rates and income levels for Japan. The table first indicates actual trade data for these years. These data show a sharp rise of US imports from $33 billion to $60 billion, accompanied by slow growth in US exports to Japan from $21

---

16. See John Williamson, *The Exchange Rate System*, POLICY ANALYSES IN INTERNATIONAL ECONOMICS 5, 2d ed., rev. (Washington: Institute for International Economics, June 1985).

The estimates here apply Williamson's FEER for the yen without his special correction for the impact of liberalization of trade barriers against Japan, considering that sector-specific pressures make the elimination of these barriers unlikely even at a much stronger level for the yen.

17. For 1984 as a whole, the actual yen-dollar rate was 237.5, compared to a FEER of 194 yen per dollar. In mid-1985, the market rate was approximately 245 yen per dollar.

TABLE 2.7   US-Japan trade, actual and simulated (billion dollars and percentage)

	1980	1981	1982	1983	1984
US imports from Japan					
Actual: Reported	32.97	39.90	39.93	43.56	60.37
Equation	33.61	39.74	40.31	50.36	62.39
Hypothetical: A	33.61	40.33	41.47	43.81	51.81
B	33.61	39.92	42.86	51.45	61.96
C	33.61	40.15	39.01	42.89	52.17
US exports to Japan					
Actual: Reported	20.79	21.82	20.97	21.89	23.58
Equation	19.75	21.19	21.03	22.00	22.10
Hypothetical: A	19.75	22.58	23.91	25.45	30.06
B	19.75	21.32	19.29	21.29	22.85
C	19.75	22.43	26.06	26.30	25.04
Trade balance					
Actual: Reported	−12.18	−18.08	−18.97	−21.67	−36.80
Equation	−13.86	−18.55	−19.28	−28.36	−40.31
Hypothetical: A	−13.86	−17.75	−17.56	−18.37	−21.75
B	−13.86	−18.60	−23.56	−30.16	−39.11
C	−13.86	−17.71	−12.94	−16.59	−23.13
Total trade, US					
Exports	220.79	233.74	212.28	200.54	217.89
Imports	256.98	273.35	254.88	269.88	341.18
Turnover	477.77	507.09	467.16	470.42	559.07
US-Japan trade balance as percentage of US turnover					
Actual: Reported	−2.55	−3.57	−4.06	−4.61	−6.58
Equation	−2.90	−3.66	−4.13	−6.03	−7.21
Hypothetical: A	−2.90	−3.50	−3.76	−3.91	−3.89
B	−2.90	−3.66	−5.04	−6.41	−7.00
C	−2.90	−3.49	−2.77	−3.53	−4.14

Note: A = hypothetical exchange rate and Japanese growth; B = hypothetical Japanese growth only; C = hypothetical exchange rate only.

billion to $24 billion and a resulting surge in the bilateral deficit from $12 billion to $37 billion. These historical levels of trade are indicated as "actual: reported."

Next the table indicates the levels of trade expected on the basis of the trade equations estimated in appendix B, under actual macroeconomic conditions. In these equations, US imports from Japan depend on US income; the dollar price of imports from Japan relative to domestic US wholesale prices (which in turn depends on domestic inflation in Japan, the nominal dollar-yen exchange rate, and the degree of pass-through of exchange rate changes to Japan's export prices); the exchange rate between the yen and other major currencies; industrial capacity in Japan; and the cyclical state of the economy, in both the United States and Japan. US exports to Japan depend on Japanese income, the real yen-dollar exchange rate (nominal rate adjusted for domestic inflation in both countries), the cyclical state of both economies, and a shift ("dummy") variable for years before 1971 reflecting greater protection in that period. Applying these equations to the actual values for exchange rates and income yields the expected trade levels labeled in table 2.7 as "actual: equation."

As shown in the table, the "equation" estimates closely follow the "reported" actual trade levels.[18] The import equation shows an expected rise of imports from $33.6 billion in 1980 (almost the same as the actual value) to $62.4 billion in 1984 (a slight overestimate), while the export equation closely tracks the slow growth of exports in this period. The trade equations predict a rise of the bilateral deficit from $13.9 billion in 1980 to $40.3 billion in 1984. Thus, the predicted deterioration of the trade balance from 1980 to 1984 is $26.5 billion, slightly larger than the actual deterioration of $24.6 billion.

A central implication of these results is that *the rise in the US-Japanese trade deficit from 1980 to 1984 can be fully explained by changes in the*

---

18. Except for imports in 1983, the trade values predicted by the model are all within 6 percent of actual values, with the average absolute value of deviation at 2.7 percent. Imports predicted for 1983 exceed the actual level by 15.1 percent in value terms and 12.7 percent in physical volume. The high import estimate for 1983 is driven by the lagged effect of a large real depreciation of the yen in 1982, and relatively large increases in US income and Japan's industrial capacity. (See table B-1, appendix B.) These results suggest that the lag structures for real import price increases should perhaps be spread out further (with some of the effect of the 1982 yen depreciation delayed until 1984), and that the elasticity for Japan's industrial capacity may be overstated.

exchange rate and rates of economic growth. There is little if any room left to attribute the rising deficit to increased protection in Japan. (Neither is there indication of any impact from Japanese trade liberalization during the period.)

The principal developments in the bilateral balance of the period 1980–84 appear to have been as follows. First, the great bulk of the deterioration occurred on the import side. In current dollar terms, US imports from Japan rose by 83.1 percent from 1980 to 1984. Exports did not decline but actually rose modestly (by 13.4 percent in value, almost solely from inflation in US export prices). Second, the rise in imports came in two broad waves. The first wave brought imports to a higher plateau in 1981–82 (a 21 percent rise above 1980 in 1981). The second wave was the surge from 1983 to 1984 (38.6 percent in current value).

The sources of these import increases were the following. In 1981, US imports rose briskly as the result of substantial appreciation in the real value of the dollar relative to the yen—and therefore a decline in the real price of imports—in both 1981 and 1980. In addition, US income growth and industrial capacity expansion in Japan boosted imports as well. In 1982, the sharp further real appreciation of the dollar relative to the yen would have meant a major increase in imports if nothing else had happened, but the severe decline in US cyclical demand and GNP level reduced potential import demand and neutralized the upward pressure from a strengthening dollar. By 1983 and especially 1984, however, the ongoing import pressure from dollar appreciation was augmented by a boost to import demand from US domestic growth and return to a high cyclical level of activity. Although there was a moderating effect on US imports in 1984 from Japan's cyclical recovery, the strong expansion in Japan's industrial capacity in 1984 more than offset this influence.

Table B-1 in appendix B sets forth the percentage contribution of each of the economic variables to annual import expansion in the period 1981–84. In broad terms, the sharp rise in US imports from Japan by 1984 may be attributed primarily to the large appreciation of the dollar relative to the yen in real terms. That this appreciation had already occurred by 1982, whereas the most impressive surge in imports did not occur until 1984, is explained by the lagged effect of the exchange rate and by the temporary depression of import demand from severe US recession in 1982.

It is possible to apply the same trade model to estimate the trade patterns that would have occurred if the dollar had not been overvalued and Japanese growth had been higher. The "hypothetical" levels of the exchange rate (fundamental equilibrium rate) and Japanese growth from table 2.6 are applied to the equations of appendix B, to obtain the "hypothetical" trade estimates in table 2.7. Case A of the hypothetical estimates refers to trade levels with the exchange rate at fundamental equilibrium and with Japan's growth at the hypothetical level; in case B only Japan's GNP differs from actual values while in case C only the exchange rate is different from actual values.

In case A, by 1984, US imports from Japan are approximately $10 billion (16.4 percent) lower than their (simulated) actual level. Without macroeconomic distortions, especially in the exchange rate (as analyzed below), US imports from Japan would have risen in value by 54 percent instead of 86 percent from 1980 to 1984. In terms of physical volume—which may be more relevant for the domestic job-dislocation effect of imports—imports would have risen by only 35 percent instead of their actual (simulated) increase of 93 percent.

The model shows adjustment on the export side as well. Actual US exports to Japan rose by only 12 percent in value and declined by 3 percent in physical volume from 1980 to 1984 (simulated basis). Under the hypothetical equilibrium conditions (case A), US exports to Japan would have risen by 52 percent in value and by 32 percent in physical volume over this same period. Figure 2.1 compares the actual (recorded) trade values with the hypothetical estimates, and shows that through both lower imports and higher exports there would have been lower trade deficits under the hypothetical macroeconomic conditions (especially by 1984).[19] With the changes on both the import and export sides, the hypothetical bilateral trade deficit by 1984 is only $21.8 billion, or lower than the simulated actual trade deficit ($40.3 billion) by $18.6 billion. This hypothetical level is in the middle of the range identified in the previous section as the structural bilateral deficit that may be expected because of Japan's "normal" current account surplus and triangular trade ($20 billion to $25 billion after the price effects of dollar correction are taken into account).

As indicated in table 2.7, the actual bilateral trade deficit rose from 2.55 percent of total US imports plus exports ("turnover") in 1980 to 6.58 percent

---

19. Because this figure compares recorded (instead of "equation" or simulated) actual values to the hypothetical values, the degree of trade imbalance correction is probably understated in 1983 (when the equation-based value for "actual" imports substantially exceeds recorded actual imports, so that the difference between "actual" and "hypothetical" imports is greater on the equation basis than suggested in the figure).

FIGURE 2.1   **US-Japanese bilateral trade, 1980–84: actual and at
equilibrium exchange rates and normal growth differentials**

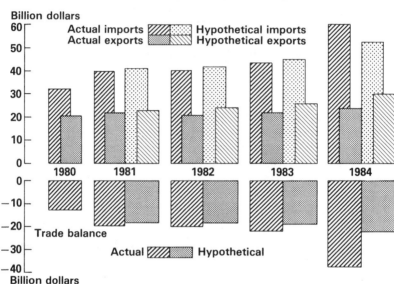

Source: Table 2.7.

in 1984. The hypothetical deficit (case A) shows a much smaller rise, from
2.90 percent of trade turnover to 3.89 percent. Nonetheless, even this smaller
rise amounts to an increase of one-third in the equilibrium bilateral trade
deficit relative to trade turnover. This upward trend reflects the fact that,
with virtually identical income elasticities of US and Japanese imports from
each other (appendix B), combined with the fact that the US export base is
little more than one-third its base of imports from Japan, there is an underlying
trend for the bilateral trade deficit to rise relative to trade volume. The
triangular nature of the trade means that US exports to third countries tend
to rise to make up the difference (as Japan spends its export earnings on
imports from other countries that in turn import from the United States). But
a modest structural trend toward a rising relative bilateral deficit (from a
much lower base after dollar correction, however) could be a longer term
feature of US-Japanese trade. This possibility is increased by the statistically
strong supply-side influence on Japan's exports associated with expanding

industrial capacity, as discussed in appendix B. These factors suggest the need for the political perception of the bilateral trade imbalance to be informed by an understanding of the basic economic forces at work in the longer term, even after correction of the macroeconomic distortions of recent years.

Even without considering any longer term trend in the bilateral deficit, under two different approaches we find a sizable US-Japan bilateral imbalance after correction of the dollar. The structural analysis above, focusing on trade triangularity and a continued (but reduced) current account surplus for Japan, yields a "normal" bilateral deficit range of $20 billion to $25 billion. The trade modeling approach (appendix B and table 2.7) finds that, at equilibrium exchange rates and normal relative growth, the 1984 bilateral deficit would have been $22 billion.

A bilateral deficit in the range of $20 billion to $25 billion would loom relatively large for a US external account with overall trade and current accounts in deficit only by about $12 billion (Williamson's equilibrium exchange rate case). Indeed, it would mean that, whereas the US trade deficit with the rest of the world would disappear entirely, that with Japan would be cut only by about half. Moreover, the United States in equilibrium would run a significant surplus with the rest of the world to offset partially its deficit with Japan. It is important that, in setting goals for correction of the present trade imbalances, the relatively large US-Japan bilateral imbalance even under equilibrium conditions be kept in mind. Otherwise there will tend to be both disappointment about results in bilateral trade with Japan and continuing pressure for protection on grounds of seemingly unfair trade results.[20]

Finally, it is possible to separate the influence of the exchange rate from that of income growth by considering the two alternative cases B and C in the calculations of hypothetical trade performance (table 2.7). In case C, the exchange rate is set at its hypothetical FEER, while Japan's income is at its actual historical levels in 1980–84. This case shows US import and export levels by 1984 that are almost identical to those estimated in the initial hypothetical case A in which not only is the exchange rate at the FEER level but, in addition, Japanese growth is first lower and subsequently higher than

---

20. It is possible that Williamson's estimate of the equilibrium exchange rate for Japan understates the extent of yen appreciation needed to reach equilibrium. In that case, the structural bilateral deficit would be somewhat lower than the $22 billion estimate identified here.

the actual level (maintaining the recent historical average spread above the US growth rate).

By contrast, in case B, the exchange rate is set at its actual level while Japan's income is set at the hypothetical level. In this case imports and exports by 1984 are almost identical to their "actual" (equation-predicted) levels. These calculations show that by far the dominant influence in the widening US Japanese deficit has been the overvaluation of the dollar rather than slow growth in Japan's income.[21] This finding is not surprising considering the small difference between the actual and hypothetical growth rates for Japan (0.4 percent annual average). Indeed, because the hypothetical growth approach states Japan's growth rate at a constant 1.8 percentage points above US growth, the hypothetical level for Japan's growth in 1982 is lower than the actual level, causing US exports to Japan in 1982 and 1983 to be lower under hypothetical growth (case B) than under actual conditions (actual: equation).

Two principal conclusions emerge from this analysis.

First, the main driving force behind the growing imbalance in the bilateral US-Japanese trade relationship has been the overvaluation of the dollar.[22] The modest relative slowdown in Japan's growth has had much less impact.

---

21. The strong influence of the exchange rate is also found in econometric research by Petri. His statistical estimates indicate that a 10 percent real appreciation of the trade-weighted dollar causes a decline of 1.4 percent in US exports to Japan and a rise of 13.8 percent in US imports from Japan. On a 1980 base, he calculates that a 10 percent rise in the dollar (against a basket of the other major currencies) causes the overall US current account to deteriorate by $20.4 billion, and the bilateral US account with Japan to decline by $4.6 billion. Considering that the dollar appreciated by 40 percent from 1980 to 1984 (Williamson), Petri's model would have predicted a deterioration in the total US current account by $81.6 billion (compared with an actual decline of $102 billion, also affected by the "growth gap" and developing-country debt crisis), and in the bilateral balance with Japan by $18.4 billion (versus an actual deterioration of $24.6 billion).

Petri's research shows a strong mirror-image relationship in the two countries' accounts. After taking account of extra exports by Japan to the rest of the world as other countries export more to an appreciating United States, and incorporating Japan's need for additional imports to produce exports, Petri finds that a 10 percent appreciation of the dollar causes Japan's current account balance to rise by $6.7 billion. The indirect net exports to third countries contribute about half as much as increased direct exports to the United States. Peter A. Petri, *Modeling Japanese–American Trade,* p. 100; and John Williamson, *The Exchange Rate System,* p. 99.

22. Another important conclusion, which is essential to our policy recommendations, is that exchange rate changes *do* translate into price changes in Japan and thus importantly affect

Second, because the bulk of the rise in imports can be explained by the macroeconomic influences of exchange rates and different rates of economic growth, there is little if any scope for increasing Japanese protection to have played a role in the rising trade imbalance.

These conclusions have important implications for the issue of protection. The groundswell of pressure for protective "retaliation" against Japan implicitly assumes one of three circumstances. The first case would be that increased Japanese protection is responsible for the increased bilateral deficit. The results here reject that hypothesis.

The second case would be that, although Japanese protection has not increased, it is no longer tolerable for the United States to permit the original level of Japanese protection in a new environment of large US deficits because the amount by which the *level* of Japanese protection suppresses US exports is extremely large and the removal of this protection by itself would go far to eliminate the bilateral trade deficit. This case, in turn, is thrown in doubt by the analysis in chapter 3.

The third case is that, even though the magnitude of Japanese protection is limited relative to the size of the bilateral deficit, the existence of the deficit provides leverage to force Japan to eliminate its protection. One can readily understand the tactical appeal of using the deficit to push for long-desired sector-specific changes. But there is a danger in selling "tough" legislation to the public on the grounds that a rollback in Japanese protection will deal importantly with the bilateral deficit, even though more sophisticated policymakers and legislators recognize that such a result is highly unlikely.[23] Even if Japan did everything asked of it, a large imbalance would remain and frustrations would intensify. The problem would be heightened. Clear

---

Japanese exports and imports. See Petri, cited above, and numerous earlier studies on the subject that have reached a similar conclusion; for a summary see Morris Goldstein and Mohsin S. Khan, "Income and Price Effects in International Trade," in *Handbook of International Economics,* edited by Peter B. Kenen and Ronald W. Jones (Amsterdam: North Holland Press, 1983).

23. In introducing the mandatory version of the Senate bill to retaliate if Japan does not provide compensatory liberalization to offset increased US auto imports (chapter 1), for example Senator Packwood stated: "We all recognize that the entire trade imbalance, or even most of the imbalance with Japan, is not attributable to Japanese import barriers." Statement of Senator Bob Packwood (R-Ore.), *Congressional Record,* vol. 131, no. 90, 9 July 1985, S.9185.

separation between the macroeconomic and sector-specific dimensions of the issue is thus critical for policy, as well as intellectual, reasons.

We have stressed, however, that the sector-specific issues must be dealt with as well. We turn now to a detailed examination of those questions, and how they might best be addressed.

3 Protection

The analysis of chapter 2 suggests that the bulk of the sharp deterioration in the US-Japan bilateral trade balance can be explained by macroeconomic factors (overvalued dollar, rapid US recovery, imbalance in both countries between saving and resource use for investment and fiscal deficits). There is little remaining role for Japanese protection to have played in causing the *increase* in the bilateral imbalance. And we have noted repeatedly that changes in trade policy cannot be expected to have major impact on the trade imbalance.

Nonetheless, US tolerance of the existing *level* of protection in Japan has declined sharply as the bilateral deficit has risen. Moreover, there is widespread feeling—in other countries as well as the United States—that Japan is simply not liberalizing its markets fast enough in light of its rapid emergence as a global economic power and major beneficiary of the world trading system (as well as a chronic surplus country). It is thus important to examine the level of protection in Japan, and to assess its quantitative impact on the overall balances as well as its sector-specific effects. We will also compare Japanese protection with that in the United States, considering that many of the demands for action against Japan are based on the premise that the Japanese market is far more protected than the US market.

This chapter first reviews quantitative evidence on overt protection: tariffs and tangible nontariff barriers. Because of the widespread view that much of Japan's protection is invisible rather than overt, whereas most US protection is quite transparent, the analysis then examines intangible protection, reviewing the arguments that contend this protection is severe in Japan and examining indirect economic evidence (using international comparisons) for empirical tests of the hypothesis that the Japanese market is more highly protected than the markets of other major industrial countries. The discussion addresses the concern that Japan may also have achieved protection of its market by manipulating its exchange rate. The chapter concludes with an evaluation of overall Japanese protection as reflected in US negotiators' objectives, and

53

TABLE 3.1   **Average tariffs in the United States and Japan, post-Tokyo Round rates[a] (percentage)**

	United States	Japan
Industrial products		
GATT definition		
W	4.4	2.8
S	6.3	6.0
UN definition[b]		
W	4.6	6.8[c]
Raw materials		
W	0.2	0.5
S	1.8	1.4
Semimanufactures		
W	3.0	4.6
S	6.1	6.3
Finished manufactures		
W	5.7	6.0
S	7.0	6.4
Selected product sectors[d]		
3112 Dairy	7.4	32.9
3113 Preserved fruits and vegetables	10.0	19.5
3116 Grain mill products	2.6	10.4
3117 Bakery	0.0	31.3
3118 Sugar	6.0	38.7
3131 Spirits	4.4	53.3
3132 Wine	7.6	59.2
3133 Malt liquors	3.0	12.7

compares this protection with that in the United States to judge the question of "reciprocity."

Overt Protection

Protection in the traditional form of tariffs is generally low in Japan as well as the United States as the consequence of the succession of postwar rounds of multilateral trade negotiations. Tariff rates following cuts negotiated in

	United States	Japan
3134 Soft drinks	0.5	32.2
3140 Tobacco	13.0	354.3^e
3211 Textile spinning	11.0	5.6
3212 Made-up textiles	19.6	12.4
3213 Knitting	14.4	12.5
3214 Carpets, rugs	6.4	11.3
3220 Apparel	22.4	13.9
3233 Leather products	13.4	11.1
3240 Footwear	9.0	14.5
3559 Rubber products n.e.c.^f	12.1	11.6
3620 Glass	10.5	5.1
3691 Clay	15.9	3.6

Note: W = import-weighted average; S = simple average.

Source: GATT, The Tokyo Round of Multilateral Trade Negotiations, vol. 2, Supplementary Report (Geneva: GATT, 1980); William R. Cline, Exports of Manufactures from Developing Countries: Performance and Prospects for Market Access (Washington: Brookings Institution, 1984), p. 52; and calculations from data tapes provided by the Office of the US Trade Representative.

a. For the United States, post–Tokyo Round cuts are to be fully phased in by 1987. For Japan, the cuts were completed by 1983.

b. The GATT definition is narrower, and excludes processed foods, copper, and certain other items. See Cline, Exports of Manufactures, p. 215.

c. Excludes tobacco products.

d. Four-digit International Standard Industrial Classification (ISIC) sectors with average tariffs of 10 percent or higher in either country. Note: There are 81 four-digit ISIC sectors.

e. Prior to subsequent reduction. See text.

f. Not elsewhere classified.

the Tokyo Round of the 1970s are shown in table 3.1. The aggregate tariff rates, either weighted (W) by imports or simple (S) averages over the thousands of tariff categories, all show low and approximately comparable tariff protection in the two countries. For industrial goods, Japan's average tariff is somewhat lower than that for the United States, using the General Agreement on Tariffs and Trade (GATT) definition of manufactures, but somewhat higher, using the broader United Nations definition based on industrial production categories (including processed foods and copper).

TABLE 3.2 **Overt nontariff barriers, Japan and United States**

| | | Percentage of manufactures[a] | |
| | | Import weights (percentage) | Consumption weights (percentage) |
Sector	Type		
Japan			
3111 Meat	Q, L	7.5	1.2
3112 Dairy	ST, L	0.9	1.1
3113 Preserved fruits and vegetables	L	1.2	0.5
3114 Canned fish	L, V	9.5	2.1
3116 Grain mill products	L	1.3	0.8
3140 Tobacco	ST	1.3	1.4
3231 Tanneries	L	3.9	0.1
3240 Footwear	L	0.4	0.3
Subtotal, narrow measure		25.8	7.4
3832 Radio, TV communications	L	3.0	4.0
3522 Drugs	L	2.6	1.7
3843 Motor vehicles	S	2.0	8.7
Total, broad measure		33.5	21.8
Total, preferred measure		31.5	13.1
United States			
3111 Meat	Q	1.9	3.8
3112 Dairy	Q	0.4	2.0

The table also reports average tariffs at the industry level for manufacturing sectors with tariffs of 10 percent or higher in either country. High-tariff categories for Japan tend to be in the processed food sectors (including the exceptionally high tariff on tobacco products).[1] In contrast, the high-tariff sectors for the United States tend to be in the textile and apparel industries and other light manufactures. US protection of over 20 percent for apparel is by far the highest in either country among manufacturing sectors outside of processed agricultural products. However, among the high-tariff sectors, Japan's protection of processed agricultural goods exceeds US protection by a wider margin than US protection of other manufactures exceeds that of Japan.

1. Note, however, that subsequent tariff reductions not reflected in table 3.1 have cut the tariff on tobacco products to 20 percent. US Department of Commerce, by communication.

| Sector | Type | Percentage of manufactures[a] | |
		Import weights (percentage)	Consumption weights (percentage)
3118 Sugar	Q	0.5	0.3
3119 Confectionery	Q	1.4	0.6
3211–19 Textiles	Q	2.0	3.5
3220 Apparel	Q	4.8	2.8
3710 Iron and steel	Q	7.4	5.7
3841 Shipbuilding	O	0.2	0.6
Subtotal, narrow measure		18.6	19.2
3240 Footwear	OMA	1.4	0.4
3832 Radio, TV communications	OMA	7.3	4.0
3843 Motor vehicles	V	17.8	10.4
Total, broad measure		45.1	34.0
Total, preferred measure		35.4	29.6

Note: Q = quotas; L = discretionary licensing; ST = state trading; S = standards; OMA = orderly marketing agreement; V = voluntary export restraint; O = other.
Source: Cline, *Exports of Manufactures from Developing Countries,* pp. 56–59 and underlying data.
a. Excluding refined oil, ISIC 3530. Weights are for 1978.

In sum, although high-tariff rates do remain in some politically sensitive categories, tariffs are no longer the dominant form of protection, and their average level is low in both the United States and Japan.

Nontariff barriers have thus become the most important form of protection. These barriers are more difficult to quantify than tariffs. Conceptually, they may be measured in terms of "tariff equivalents" by examining the extent to which they raise the domestic price above the world price. In practice, data are rarely available to measure tariff equivalents.

Table 3.2 presents estimates of the breadth of coverage of major overt nontariff barriers (NTBs) on manufactured products in Japan and the United States. (Japan is highly protective on a number of important agricultural products, to which we turn later in analyzing the prospects for increased US exports.) These barriers include import quotas, "voluntary" export restraints, orderly marketing arrangements, discretionary licensing, and (in the case of Japan) state trading. The data in the table indicate the percentage of the total market for manufactured goods (broad definition, including processed foods) covered by sectors in which these NTBs exist.

The table presents two alternative measures. The preferred measure indicates the share of each protected sector in total domestic consumption of manufactures. An alternative measure reports each protected sector's share in total imports of manufactures.[2] The import basis refers to all imports of the product in question, even if protection applies only to a limited set of suppliers, on the grounds that protection against a major supplier acts as a potential threat to others and discourages their expansion of exports to the market as well.[3] Neither the import-based measure nor that based on consumption shares addresses the issue of the severity of protection. Instead, these measures simply indicate whether the sectors covered by NTBs are large or small in economic terms.

Table 3.2 shows a significant difference between the form of NTB protection in Japan and that in the United States. In most cases, the discretionary license is the form of protection in Japan.[4] By contrast, outright import quotas and "voluntary" export quotas (and "orderly marketing arrangements") dominate NTB protection in the United States.

The table presents narrow and broad alternative measures of protection for both countries. In the case of Japan, the three sectors added under the broad measure do not appear as protected in the underlying data base compiled by Cline from GATT and other sources.[5] However, Balassa and Balassa report that Japan applies discretionary licensing in telecommunications equipment

---

2. Weighting by imports usually tends to understate protection, because the import volume of highly protected sectors tends to be depressed by that protection. Ironically, the import weighting shows larger market coverage by nontariff barriers (NTBs) than does consumption weighting. This pattern suggests a process in which high imports eventually trigger protection, rather than the reverse case in which preexisting protection suppresses imports.

3. That such a risk is real is illustrated by the extension of US quotas on steel to a large number of developing countries in 1984, following the quota regime on European steel implemented in 1982.

4. Outright quotas on manufactured goods in Japan are de minimus, applying only to coal briquettes and leather products. Gary R. Saxonhouse, "The Micro- and Macroeconomics of Foreign Sales to Japan," in *Trade Policy in the 1980s,* edited by William R. Cline (Washington: Institute for International Economics, 1983), pp. 259–304.

5. Cline, *Exports of Manufactures from Developing Countries,* pp. 43–63.

and pharmaceuticals. They also argue that Japanese product standards have been applied in a protectionist manner for automobiles.[6] But Japan's obvious success in international competition in the automobile sector casts doubt on the need for, and meaning of, such protection.

The measures shown in table 3.2 indicate that between 7 percent and 33 percent of the Japanese market for manufactures is covered by overt NTBs. (Agricultural raw materials are not included in the table.) Perhaps the best range would be that based on the broader concept but excluding automobiles, meaning that between 13.1 percent of the manufactures market (consumption basis) and 31.5 percent (import basis) is protected by overt NTBs in Japan. Averaging these figures in turn, approximately one-fifth to one-fourth of the Japanese market is protected by these barriers.

In the case of the United States, the narrow and broad alternatives refer to time periods rather than ambiguity about presence of protection. The broad definition includes all sectors that have experienced NTB protection since the late 1970s. The narrow definition excludes those sectors on which protection has been phased out as of mid-1985: color television sets, footwear, and (arguably) automobiles.

But the distinction between the broad and narrow groupings is ambiguous even at the present time. The Reagan administration rejected footwear protection in August 1985, despite a finding of import injury by the US International Trade Commission (USITC), but the threat of congressional action remains. While quotas on television sets from the late 1970s had lapsed, the constant threat of protection in this sector had induced a new strategy of direct investment by Japanese and Korean producers in the United States, not unlike the process whereby US manufacturers invested within Europe in an earlier period to get behind the protective tariff wall of the Common Market. In automobiles, Japanese authorities expressly limited the increase in exports in 1985 to 24 percent. Although the Reagan administration professed to be displeased that controls were not totally removed on Japanese automobile exports once the US decision to liberalize was taken in March 1985, the political-economic reality was such that complete liberalization would have precipitated an even angrier congressional response than actually occurred.

On balance, we opt for continuing the inclusion of automobiles in the

---

6. Bela Balassa and Carol Balassa, "Industrial Protection in Developed Countries," *The World Economy,* vol. 7, no. 2 (June 1984), p. 185.

measurement of protected sectors in the United States, but omit footwear and television as not currently protected. On this basis, the fraction of the US market for manufactures protected by NTBs ranges between 29.6 percent (consumption basis) and 36.4 percent (import basis), for a simple average of 33.0 percent.

In sum, one-fifth to one-fourth of the Japanese market for manufactures is protected by overt NTBs, while one-third of the American market is protected by such measures.[7] These estimates are inherently imprecise, and they have two major shortcomings. Because comparable data are not available, the estimates of table 3.2 do not include raw agricultural products, in which Japan is more protective than the United States. However, subsequent analysis in this chapter explicitly considers the quantitative impact of the principal cases of agricultural protection in Japan (rice, beef, and citrus fruits). Neither do the estimates of trade coverage by nontariff barriers address the relative severity of these restraints in the two countries. Nonetheless, the estimates cast doubt on the common view that the Japanese market is far more protected than the US market, a premise that underlies the congressional wave of ''reciprocity'' initiatives urging retaliation against Japan because of excessively high protection.[8]

---

7. Note that even if automobiles are *included* in Japan's protection and *excluded* in US protection, the two markets show comparable protective coverage (21.8 percent and 19.2 percent, respectively, on the consumption basis).

8. See William R. Cline, *''Reciprocity'': A New Approach to World Trade Policy?* POLICY ANALYSES IN INTERNATIONAL ECONOMICS 2 (Washington: Institute for International Economics, September 1982).

Note that Staiger, Deardorff, and Stern have presented extremely rough ''guesstimates'' of the tariff-equivalent of nontariff barriers in Japan and the United States (apparently including, in the case of Japan, tacit as well as overt NTBs). Many of these data are from periods as early as 1973, and their translation of the fraction of trade covered by NTBs to tariff-equivalents appears primarily intuitive. Moreover, they indicate such anomalies as identical tariff-equivalents (10 percent) for US and Japanese NTBs on transport material.

However, they imply that the incidence of NTB protection in Japan is roughly comparable to that in the United States even though the estimates apparently go beyond overt barriers. For nonfood manufacturing, the simple average tariff-equivalent in 15 broad product sectors (three-digit International Standard Industrial Classification, ISIC, categories) for the United States is 9.3 percent; for Japan, the average is 14.1 percent if petroleum products (66 percent) are included, and 10.4 percent excluding that sector.

Similarly, the authors' various simulations with a large econometric model of trade find that the effects of US protection on Japan's trade are broadly comparable to those of Japan's protection on US trade (although the simulations do find that, in Japan, NTB protection is more

Recent estimates by the World Bank provide additional evidence supporting our qualitative conclusion that overt nontariff barriers are no more extensive in Japan than in the United States. Using data on nontariff barriers submitted by exporting countries to GATT and compiled by the United Nations Conference on Trade and Development (UNCTAD), the authors estimate that in 1983 the United States protected 17.3 percent of its total nonfuel imports, while Japan protected 16.9 percent.[9] The authors did find Japan more protective in agriculture, with 42.9 percent of agricultural imports covered by NTBs in contrast to 24.2 percent for the United States. However, much higher NTB coverage by the United States than by Japan in several key industrial sectors[10] brought the measure of protection in total manufacturing to a significantly higher level for the United States (17.1 percent NTB

---

important relative to tariff protection). The key exception to comparability between the two countries is in primary products, with Japanese tariff-equivalents of 97 percent for agricultural goods and 75 percent for processed foods (versus 32 percent in the United States). Robert W. Staiger, Alan V. Deardorff, and Robert M. Stern, "The Effects of Protection on the Factor Content of Japanese and American Foreign Trade" (Ann Arbor: University of Michigan, 29 March 1985; processed).

Other recent estimates find tariff-equivalents of NTBs far lower for both the United States and Japan. Citing estimates in a Harvard doctoral dissertation by C. G. Turner, Petri places the 1980 tariff-equivalent of Japan's quantitative restrictions at only 5.1 percent for agricultural and food products and only 3.1 percent on average for all industries. The US average is even lower, at 0.9 percent. However, these estimates appear too low to be reliable; US textile and apparel quotas are estimated to have a tariff-equivalent of only 1.3 percent. Peter A. Petri, *Modeling Japanese–American Trade: A Study of Asymmetric Interdependence* (Cambridge, Mass.: Harvard University Press, 1984), p. 138.

9. Julio J. Noguès, Andrzej Olechowski, and L. Alan Winters, "The Extent of Non-Tariff Barriers to Industrial Countries' Imports," World Bank Discussion Paper DRD115 (Washington, January 1985), p. 43. Figures cited here are for estimates weighted by each country's own imports. Note that the World Bank includes as protected only imports from suppliers specifically restricted, not imports from all sources in a protected sector. This treatment explains why the World Bank estimates for manufactures are somewhat lower than those of table 3.2. Note also that the study attributes high protection to the United States in fuels (100 percent NTB coverage); total NTB coverage including fuel is 43.0 percent for the United States and 11.9 percent for Japan. The study cites licensing of natural gas, oil, and petroleum products in the United States. However, we would not view US import policy in fuels as protective (since the removal of quotas on oil in 1973).

10. US and Japanese NTB coverage estimates (respectively) are: textiles, 57.0 percent and 11.8 percent; footwear, 11.5 percent and 34.1 percent; iron and steel, 37.7 percent and 0.0 percent; electrical machinery, 52 percent and 0.0 percent; vehicles, 34.2 percent and 0.0 percent; and other manufactures, 6.1 percent and 7.7 percent. *Ibid.*

coverage) than for Japan (7.7 percent), causing the total nonfuel measure to be marginally higher for the United States as well.

Another area of overt protection concerns one particular aspect of *export controls*: the embargo on US exports of Alaskan oil. The legislation that authorized construction of the Trans-Alaska oil pipeline prohibited exports of oil carried by the pipeline. At the present time, this oil is shipped to West Coast markets, and some of it is shipped through the Panama Canal to refineries on the Gulf Coast. Some analysts estimate that US exports to Japan could rise by $16 billion annually merely by the elimination of this export embargo on North Slope oil.[11] Others contend that about one half of the 1.7 million barrels a day produced in these fields already goes to natural markets on the West Coast, and that only the remaining half would be available for export to Japan. These analysts also argue that in any event Japan would limit its purchases of North Slope oil (presumably to maintain its trade relations with suppliers in the Organization of Petroleum Exporting Countries, OPEC), holding imports to as little as 200,000 barrels a day ($2 billion annually).[12] A careful analysis by the Federal Trade Commission (FTC) estimates that lifting the export ban would cause an increase in US exports of oil to Japan in the amount of 823,000 barrels a day, or $8.1 billion annually.[13]

Liberalization of oil exports from Alaska is politically difficult because it would tend to raise oil prices in California, and because US oil tankers currently enjoy a monopoly on coastal shipping (under the Jones Act) while exports to Japan would tend to be shipped in internationally competitive vessels. Liberalization might also have implications for world oil prices. In the first instance, it would tend to reduce OPEC sales to Japan while increasing US imports, perhaps primarily from Mexico. However, this measure, fully under US control, would appear to have the scope for increasing US exports by at least two-fifths to one-third of the amount by which trade barriers in Japan currently limit US exports (low estimate of $2 billion in potential oil exports, compared to central estimate later in this chapter of $5 billion to $8 billion for the adverse effect of Japanese tangible and intangible import barriers on US exports). If the FTC estimate is correct, new exports of

11. *Wall Street Journal*, 8 April 1985.

12. *Journal of Commerce*, 10 June 1985.

13. Calvin T. Rousch, Jr., *The Benefits of Eliminating the Alaskan Crude Oil Export Ban* (Washington: Federal Trade Commission, August 1984). The quantity of oil shifted from the Gulf Coast market would be 800,000 barrels a day, and from California an average of 23,000 barrels a day (pp. 22–23, 31–32). At $27 a barrel, annual exports to Japan would be $8.1 billion.

Alaskan oil from US liberalization would equal or exceed the probable increase in all other exports to Japan that would result from thoroughgoing import liberalization by Japan.[14]

Liberalizing Alaskan oil exports would of course have little effect on the global trade balance of the United States or Japan. New US exports to Japan would be offset by new US imports from Mexico and elsewhere, and Japan's new imports from the United States would reduce its imports from OPEC. However, a working hypothesis of this study is that US-Japan trade conflict rises with the relative size of the bilateral trade deficit. A reduction in the bilateral deficit could help defuse trade conflict even without any change in the global trade balance of either country.[15]

Intangible Protection

Even though overt tariff and nontariff barriers to trade seem to be no higher in Japan than in the United States, at least on manufactured products, it is widely believed that the Japanese market is in practice more highly protected than markets in the United States and Europe. Informed observers tend to agree that, to the extent Japanese protection is significantly higher than in other industrial countries, the difference is attributable to intangible forms of protection rather than tariffs and overt NTBs.

GOVERNMENT PROCUREMENT

The Japanese government is often viewed by US businessmen and trade negotiators as discriminating against imports in its own procurement. The

---

14. The point is sometimes made that the US export controls are not the decisive problem for US-Japan oil trade, because they cover only Alaskan crude oil and it is Japan that refuses to import refined petroleum products. However, because of the lead phase-down program, gasoline is now in short supply in the United States and we have become an importer of the product. The only petroleum product available for export from the US West Coast is residual fuel oil, of a type that Japan does not use. Philip K. Verleger, private communication, 11 July 1985.

15. *Past* US export controls, by raising doubts about the reliability of supplies from this country, have also increased the bilateral trade imbalance in both the short and longer runs. The most important instance was probably the US embargo on soybean sales in 1973, which inter alia promoted Japanese investment of about $1 billion in Brazil to develop an alternative source of supply for a product critical to the Japanese diet. Any US efforts to negotiate reductions of Japanese import barriers on food products, notably rice, would be further hampered by this history.

most conspicuous case has been that of Nippon Telephone and Telegraph (NTT), until recently a government entity. The USITC has cited extremely low imports by NTT as evidence that Japan did not follow the spirit of the new GATT code on government procurement in the 1980s.[16] In recent years the government has also reportedly refused to purchase US communications satellites and, until one year ago, told private firms to do the same (with the proscription still reportedly applicable to NTT).

In the face of pressure from US negotiators, top policy officials have begun to urge neutrality and even favoritism to imports in government procurement (as noted in the discussion on negotiations in chapter 1). For example, in August 1985, a senior Japanese official responded to a US request to import big-ticket items by indicating that government agencies would immediately purchase US communications satellites.[17]

REGULATION

The US Trade Representative (USTR), as well as Japan's own Keidanren business organization, have stressed the import-suppressing consequences of widespread regulation and red tape in Japan.[18] The USTR cites a celebrated case of a patent application by a US firm for optical fibers. Japanese authorities delayed approval for a decade, by which time domestic Japanese production had become available. The USTR notes that most regulations were not intended to protect the Japanese market but have had a protective effect as the economy has come into more intense contact with the rest of the world. In some cases, regulation does not comply with internationally accepted practices or standards, making compliance more costly and time consuming.

In the area of testing and standards, the USTR contends that Japan has not lived up to the spirit of the GATT Agreement on Technical Barriers to Trade (Standards Code) in acceptance of foreign test data and in transparency for the setting of standards. Thus, some Japanese ministries have not permitted

---

16. US International Trade Commission, *Foreign Industrial Targeting and the Effects on US Industries. Phase I. Japan,* USITC Publication No. 1437 (Washington, October 1983). See discussion below.

17. *Journal of Commerce,* 13 August 1985. The previous breakthrough sale of communications satellites by Hughes Aircraft in consortium with Japanese private companies reportedly reflected US negotiating pressure.

18. Office of the US Trade Representative, "US Statement on Japanese Market Access," addressed to OECD Trade Committee, 11 June 1985, and Keidanren, "Smoothing the Way for Imports: Keidanren Presses for Regulatory Reform," Keizai Koho Center Brief No. 26, Tokyo, February 1985, pp. 1–3.

factory inspections and product-type approvals by foreign testing agencies. Some foreign firms complain that products are rejected without information on how they can be changed to meet certification requirements. The USTR also charges that the government allows industry groupings to set their own regulatory standards, with protective effect.

Japan's Keidanren itself echoes some of these complaints. While rejecting as a "myth" the popular view that transactions among "family groups" make the market impenetrable (because the Japanese market is "simply too competitive to allow success based on dependence on special trading relationships") as well as the view that the Japanese distribution system itself discriminates against foreign goods, the Keidanren has singled out regulation as an area where practices with protective effect continue. It calls for fast-track procedures of import authorization for broad categories of goods not posing regulatory problems; execution of procedures at the most convenient time and place after entry rather than at the water's edge; revision of Japanese standards to adhere to internationally accepted practice (much regulation is "excessively severe"); elimination of duplicative regulation by various agencies and adoption of the most abbreviated procedures currently applied among them; simplification of documentation (including an end to the requirement that documents be reissued when foreign governments have already provided documentation); and formation of special teams to clear up backlogs.

OLIGOPOLY BEHAVIOR

Noncompetitive behavior is another sphere in which de facto protection might arise. Interrelationships among business entities are extensive in Japan, as best represented by the *keiretsu* groups that include manufacturing, trading, and financial corporations. Caves and Uekusa argue that Japan's business structure is more concentrated and oligopolistic than that in the United States. They note that the keiretsu and other business groupings may cause behavior in which member firms trade with each other at transfer prices different from those that would exist in the absence of group behavior.[19] However, the

---

19. The authors note that with monopoly power present, equilibrium price ratios do not equal ratios of marginal opportunity cost. Traders banding together might trade at shadow prices equal to marginal opportunity cost in order to maximize joint profits, and then make payments to the losing members of the group. Richard Caves and Masu Uekusa, "Industrial Organization," in *Asia's New Giant: How the Japanese Economy Works,* edited by Hugh Patrick and Henry Rosovsky (Washington: Brookings Institution, 1976), pp. 496–97.

authors draw no conclusions about the implications of Japanese business structure for tacit import protection, and indeed they suggest that oligopoly and collusion in the Japanese economy provide shelter for inefficient firms (rather than enhancing Japanese competitiveness).

The USTR cites three areas in which oligopoly behavior restrains imports. First, the government permits "recession cartels" designed to rationalize declining industries. The practical effect is to limit imports in these sectors, according to the USTR, which cites the paper industry where cartels have existed to cope with the problem of high energy and raw material costs. Second, the USTR views the distribution system as a close-knit network of financial and other arrangements linking suppliers, distributors, and customers in a fashion that excludes not only foreign suppliers but new Japanese entrants as well. Third, the USTR argues that the keiretsu conglomerates of manufacturing, banking, and foreign trading entities that support each others' activities effectively preclude opportunities for other firms.

Some reports indicate that even highly efficient and long-established Japanese firms find it difficult to break into markets controlled by traditional economic groups. Indeed, some of the outsider firms are reported to welcome US pressure for transparency in standards and other reforms in telecommunications as an opportunity to break into markets controlled by traditional "family groupings," and even seek joint ventures with American (and other foreign) firms to "ride the foreign pressure" back into their own national markets.

It is unclear, however, whether the presence of an oligopoly grouping automatically leads to protection against imports (or discrimination against nongroup Japanese suppliers). Oligopoly behavior within a group of associated firms, in its most intense form, would replicate decisions of a single large firm with the same product lines. In the long run, the single firm would maximize profits by importing inputs that are cheaper than those that can be purchased from one of its divisions (that is, from a partner firm in the case of the grouping).

Conceivably, in the short term, there could be discrimination against imports. In the short run, a single large firm would choose supplies from its own division as long as the variable cost was equal to or less than the full cost of the import (including its fixed production cost). Dynamic considerations might also change the conclusion about long-run behavior; a monopoly firm might purchase from its own division (and group members might purchase from a group partner) at a price above world levels if it expected learning curve benefits to bring costs below world prices at some time in the future.

As noted above, the Keidanren has expressed skepticism about the protective effects of industry groupings, on the ground that the Japanese market is highly competitive. Moreover, the magnitude of the keiretsu sector relative to the entire economy would suggest limits to any role it might play in restraining imports. The six largest keiretsu groups—Mitsubishi, Mitsui, Sumitomo, Fuyo, Sanwa, and DKB—accounted for only 4.9 percent of employment, although they held 15.3 percent of assets and earned 17.6 percent of net profits in the Japanese economy in 1983. The six large trading companies affiliated with these groups obtained 11.5 percent of their purchases from companies belonging to the same group as the trading company, and channeled only 4.6 percent of their sales to such companies.[20]

One celebrated case in which US producers charge that oligopolistic behavior in Japan screens out imports is that of semiconductors. In June 1985, the US Semiconductor Industry Association (SIA) petitioned the President to act under section 301 of the Trade Act of 1974.[21] The SIA argues that over the past decade the Japanese government, and then the six largest electronics firms, have acted to restrict imports of semiconductors. As evidence, the SIA argues that the US share of the Japanese market, approximately 10 percent, is far below the US share in other international markets (typically over 50 percent). The industry also maintains that the virtual constancy of the US share in the Japanese market over the last decade—despite liberalization negotiated by the United States in the early 1970s—is evidence that Japanese firms buy only a prescribed and limited share of their needs from US suppliers. The SIA contends that, even as the Japanese government liberalized formal barriers in the early 1970s, it replaced them with counterliberalization measures, instructing government agencies to buy Japanese products and urging private firms to do the same. It is also argued that the sudden disappearance of US exports to Japan in a semiconductor product, once the Japanese industry is capable of producing it, is evidence of protection because normal market mechanisms would be more likely to yield gradual market share changes.[22]

In recent years, according to the SIA, the heart of Japanese protection of

---

20. Kazuo Nukazawa, "Keiretsu: Myths and Realities" (Tokyo: Keidanren, 1985; processed).
21. Semiconductor Industry Association, *Japanese Market Barriers in Microelectronics* (San Jose, Calif.: SIA, 14 June 1985). Also see Robert J. Samuelson, "Messy Trade Problems," *Washington Post,* 28 August 1985, p. G1.
22. Michael Borrus, James Millstein, and John Zysman, *International Competition in Advanced Industrial Sectors: Trade and Development in the Semiconductor Industry,* report prepared for the Joint Economic Committee, 97 Cong., 2 sess., Washington, 1982.

semiconductors has been reciprocal buying arrangements among the six large electronics firms, arrangements originally instigated by the government of Japan. Under these arrangements Japanese firms buy their semiconductor needs primarily from each other, although larger purchases from US suppliers occur when supplies are tight. The SIA petition requests that the Japanese government force its firms to purchase more US chips, to offset discrimination. US negotiators have already pressed for such a remedy, and the SIA petition is in support of these negotiations. The industry does not seek protection, because that would raise the price of semiconductors to US computer firms, placing them at an international disadvantage and threatening the long-term viability of the prime customers of the US semiconductor industry.

The semiconductor experience is also consistent, however, with the view that increasing Japanese competitiveness is the dominant factor. The sector is subject to the same doubts concerning the "oligopoly protection" thesis as outlined above. It involves a product with dramatic dynamic comparative advantage and learning-curve benefits. As the Japanese firms accomplished efficient scale, they came to dominate the world market in the more standardized microchips (first the 64K RAM—random access memory chip— and then the 256K RAM). Increased efficiency in production in Japan could well explain any failure of the US market share in Japan to rise. In this type of product, one would not be surprised to see the sudden changes in market shares at the individual product level, cited by the US industry, as resulting from major shifts in cost of production rather than from protection.[23]

INDUSTRIAL TARGETING

Government industrial targeting is a broader area of policy intervention in Japan that is often regarded by US firms and policymakers as protective in effect. The array of instruments for targeting includes positive incentives—

---

23. This conclusion is also reached in Paul R. Krugman, "The US Response to Foreign Industrial Targeting," *Brookings Papers on Economic Activity,* no. 1, 1984, pp. 110–13. Note that the Japanese industry has contested the statistical basis of the SIA petition. The SIA maintains that the US market share in Japan is 11 percent while the Japanese market share in the United States is 17 percent. A recent study by Japan's MITI argues that these market shares are misleading because they are based on all types of semiconductors, and that in the more relevant integrated circuit (computer logic and memory chip) market the US share in the Japanese market in 1984 (including affiliate sales) was 19.1 percent, compared with a Japanese share of 9.6 percent in the US market. *Journal of Commerce* and *Washington Post,* 27 August 1985.

special financing, tax incentives, special programs of collaborative research—as well as direct protection of the domestic market and, through tools such as subsidized export finance, direct support for penetration of markets abroad.

The USITC gives a mixed review of industrial targeting in Japan,[24] noting that it was much less active after the mid-1960s. Sectors targeted in the postwar period have included electric power, coal mining, shipping, iron and steel, machinery, electronics, petroleum, automobiles, aviation, and machine tools—although strong export performance in autos and electronics was not primarily due to targeting. In recent years, targeting has focused on high technology sectors: computers, numerically controlled machine tools, and robotics. The government draws up specific plans ("visions") for targeted sectors, but leaves implementation to the private sector.

The targeting instrument of formal import protection was abandoned by the early 1970s, and government financing has been limited. However, the USITC staff singles out discriminatory government procurement as a tool of targeting, and finds that sustained government-industry ties have caused continued discrimination even after the government procurement code (negotiated in the Tokyo Round) took effect in 1981. Of large annual purchases by NTT, the largest entity covered by the code, only about 1 percent went for imports in the early 1980s. Nonetheless, the USITC study implies that the overall force of Japan's industrial targeting, and in particular its effect in protecting the domestic market, has been less than commonly thought.

In his review of industrial targeting by Japan and other industrial countries, Paul Krugman concludes that it "has not been a serious problem for the United States."[25] He notes that Japan's financial subsidies have been small, amounting to less than $100 million annually in the well-publicized case of very large integrated circuits (about the same magnitude as provided to US firms by the Department of Defense). Saxonhouse has estimated that Japan's total government subsidies to manufacturing, excluding food processing, have averaged less than 0.1 percent of value added.[26]

Krugman notes that despite the popular impression of a major Japanese assault on world markets in high technology sectors, from 1970 to 1980 the share of high technology goods in manufactured exports actually declined for Japan from 15.9 percent to 13.6 percent (mainly because medium

---

24. USITC, *Foreign Industrial Targeting.*
25. Krugman, "The US Response to Foreign Industrial Targeting," pp. 77–120.
26. Gary R. Saxonhouse, "What Is All This About 'Industrial Targeting' in Japan?" in *The World Economy*, vol. 6 (September 1983), pp. 253–74.

technology products such as automobiles were the high-growth export sectors), while it held constant for the United States (at 28 percent).[27] The Japanese export expansion was thus even more pronounced in the aggregate than in high technology goods, which remain a modest share of total exports. Krugman also argues that government subsidies to collaborative research and development would spur output and export market shares only in certain types of technology: that which has benefits that cannot be appropriated by the individual firms (otherwise the firms will do the research without government help) and at the same time generates external benefits that can be kept specifically within the country (otherwise US firms would enjoy the technological findings of Japanese research). He finds little evidence that this combination of conditions has characterized Japan's research subsidies, and cites the RAM chip as a major example of government-sponsored research that did not meet these criteria (because firms could appropriate gains, and what spillover occurred was internationally available).

Concerning the argument that Japan uses domestic protection as a springboard for subsequent export expansion, Krugman notes that, in automobiles, major protection in the Japanese market ended in the late 1950s while the surge in US imports of Japanese autos occurred only after the second oil shock, in 1979. In steel, although explicit protection did exist before 1960 and tacit restriction of the distribution system may have persisted thereafter, protection of the US market since the early 1970s has limited Japan's inroads.[28]

OTHER ARGUMENTS

Outright national preference is another characteristic sometimes attributed to the Japanese market. There may be an embedded cultural attitude that, as an

27. Krugman, "The US Response to Foreign Industrial Targeting," p. 107. High technology sectors are defined as those with ratios of R&D costs to sales more than twice the 1970 US manufacturing average.

28. Even assuming the existence of the alleged Japanese targeting practices, Bruce Scott points out in "US Competitiveness: Concepts, Performance, and Implications" that "we must distinguish successful Japanese business practices [and differences in business-government relations] . . . from unfair trade practices. . . ." Scott generally concludes that theirs is a "more effective" strategy. In "National Strategies: Key to International Competition," Scott concludes that "targeting is only part of the new strategies—and by itself is not normally a very successful part." Both papers appear in *US Competitiveness in the World Economy*, edited by Bruce R. Scott and George C. Lodge (Boston, Mass.: Harvard Business School Press, 1985), pp. 13–143.

island state with high population relative to natural resources, Japan must buy national products whenever possible. Two oil shocks and the US embargo on soybean exports in the 1970s may have contributed to the perpetuation of such sentiments. However, there is also evidence that Japanese consumer resistance to imports has more to do with perceived product quality than patriotism.[29]

The highly dispersed and labor-intensive retail distribution system is sometimes cited as an intangible barrier to imports. Foreign firms may find it difficult to sell their goods through these distribution systems. Nonetheless, there are numerous counter examples of foreign ability to penetrate the Japanese consumer market.[30]

In sum, numerous arguments in the debate on US-Japanese trade contend that tacit protection is important in Japan and that total protection greatly exceeds that from overt tariff and nontariff barriers. In the next section, we will therefore employ several techniques to try to quantify the total effect of protection in Japan—from intangible as well as overt barriers.

Before doing so, however, we would note that some of these alleged tools of Japanese protection could be remedied by government action but others involve structural traits of the society that, if present, would be difficult to eliminate by policy. The areas of protection directly under the Japanese government's control include tariffs (where high individual duties such as those on plywood and tobacco cause trade problems) and overt nontariff barriers (quotas on leather goods and numerous agricultural products). In principle, the government also has direct control over government procurement (although mid-level bureaucrats seeking to screen out imports may thwart directives of top policymakers to be more open). Regulation is another area generally subject to government control. Concerning the distribution system, the government could eliminate restrictions limiting the number and location

---

29. Susan Chira, "Can U.S. Goods Succeed in Japan?", *New York Times*, 7 April 1985.
30. Schick is the largest selling razor blade in Japan, Coca-Cola the largest selling soft drink, and Nestlé holds 70 percent of the instant coffee market. IBM employs 15,000 in its fully owned Japanese subsidiary. Major brand names in Japan include McDonalds, Kentucky Fried Chicken, Mister Donut; Del Monte, Seven-Up, Kleenex; Max Factor, Revlon, and Chanel; Bayer, BASF, and Hoechst; Cross, Shaeffer, and Parker; Pierre Cardin and Yves Saint Laurent; Adidas, Wilson, Prince, and Head. Although many of these brands are licensed, their success indicates that consumers are receptive to foreign brands. Kenichi Ohmae, *Triad Power: The Coming Shape of Global Competition* (New York: Free Press, 1985), pp. 108–9; *Wall Street Journal*, 28 June 1982.

of large retail outlets (facilitating the establishment of major US retail chains). Industrial targeting is also within the control of government, although as noted its influence in recent years has been limited and the use of formal protection for targeting purposes was phased out by the mid-1960s.

Important areas of perceived protection, however, lie beyond the control of the government. Supposed protection from oligopoly or "group" behavior would not be within the immediate grasp of the government. The "recession cartel" could be disallowed by the government but it is difficult to envision a massive break-up of the keiretsu groups, even if the government adopted antitrust legislation and policies closer to those in the United States (and even a wrenching industrial restructuring of this type might have little impact on protection, as discussed above). Similarly, any pure consumer preference for national goods would be beyond government control unless the government was prepared to grant an across-the-board subsidy to imports.

The quantitative estimates presented below for the adverse impact of Japanese protection on US exports involve both classes of protection: those within, and those beyond, government control. An attempt is then made to determine the relative importance of these two types of obstacles. We will try to assess how much of the scope for liberalization lies within the government's control, to see whether even the most energetic policy effort to liberalize would satisfy US interest groups—or leave them frustrated by meager consequences, thereby risking further aggravation of the current trade tensions.

Indirect Evidence

It is difficult to evaluate the individual types of tacit protection alleged to exist in Japan, as enumerated above. It is nonetheless possible to obtain some impression of their relevance by the use of indirect tests on overall Japanese trade, and we will employ several different techniques to that end.

IMPORT-GNP RATIOS

One such test is a comparison across countries of the ratio of imports to GNP. Large economies tend to be more self-sufficient than small economies, primarily because they have more scope for economies of scale and tend to have more diversified natural resources. Large countries thus have a lower

TABLE 3.3   **Imports of goods and nonfactor services as percentage of GNP, industrial countries (billion dollars and percentage)**

Country or area	GNP[a]	Imports/GNP[b]
United States	1,886	8.7
European Economic Community	1,412	12.8
Japan	707	12.9
Canada	177	23.3
Spain	129	16.7
Australia	79	15.9
Sweden	56	28.5
Switzerland	42	30.6
Austria	37	33.6
Finland	30	27.7
Norway	28	41.1
New Zealand	17	28.7

Source: Calculated from IMF, *International Financial Statistics,* various issues; *OECD Economic Outlook,* December 1984; and Kravis, Heston, and Summers, "Real GDP *Per Capita* for More Than One Hundred Countries."
a. 1984 GNP at 1974 real dollars, adjusted for cross-country differences in purchasing power.
b. 1974–84 average.

ratio of imports to GNP than smaller economies. If Japan's ratio of imports to GNP is sharply lower than suggested by the international pattern as related to size of the economy, one might conclude that the Japanese economy is in effect more highly protected than other major countries.

Table 3.3 shows the average ratio of imports of goods and (nonfactor) services to GNP in 1974–84 for the United States, Japan, and several other industrial countries. The countries are listed in descending order by size of GNP in 1984, stated in real terms in 1974 dollars and adjusted for international differences in purchasing power.[31] The table treats the 10 countries of the

31. Data on imports of goods and nonfactor services and on GNP, both in national currencies, are from IMF, *International Financial Statistics,* various issues. Real income for 1974 adjusted for international differences in purchasing power is from Irving B. Kravis, Alan W. Heston, and Robert Summers, "Real GDP *Per Capita* for More Than One Hundred Countries," *Economic Journal,* vol. 88, no. 350 (June 1978), pp. 215–42. (Note that the concept of purchasing power here is based on direct comparisons of product prices in sample surveys, not on the "purchasing

European Economic Community (EEC) as a single large group and reports the ratio of their imports of goods and services from outside countries (but not from each other) to their aggregate GNP, on grounds that free trade within the EEC makes the area similar to a single country in terms of the pattern of trade.[32]

As expected, the ratio of imports to GNP tends to decline as the size of GNP rises. Figure 3.1 presents these data in a scatter diagram (with a logarithmic scale for GNP). This diagram shows a clear pattern of declining imports relative to GNP as the size of GNP rises. The hypothesis of excessive protection in Japan would imply that the observation for Japan lies far below the trend line for the other countries. Instead, Japan lies extremely close to the general line relating the ratio of imports to GNP, on the one hand, to size of GNP, on the other.[33]

The diagram also suggests that the import-GNP ratio tends to be higher for European countries (adjusting for size); at an intermediate ratio for Canada and the United States; and at a lower ratio for New Zealand and Australia, other Pacific nations. This pattern is consistent with the greater facility of external trade in geographically close European countries than in distant Pacific countries, as a reflection of transport and informational costs. It may also reflect relatively high protection in New Zealand and Australia, however; the latter country is the farthest below the international line.

A more complete test allows for other important influences on the ratio of imports to GNP than just the size of the economy. Transportation costs are higher for Pacific countries because of their great distance from US and European markets, tending to reduce their import-GNP ratios.

Natural resource endowments may work in the other direction. Because of the high comparative disadvantage of producing or replacing key natural

---

power–parity'' approach of deflating a country's exchange rate movements over time by relative price indexes to some supposed equilibrium base year.) Real income for subsequent years applies series on real GNP growth (from *International Financial Statistics*) to these 1974 cross-country estimates.

32. Intra-EEC imports of nonfactor services, for which data are not directly available, are estimated based on the ratio of intra-EEC to total merchandise trade.

33. The regression line drawn in figure 3.1 is:

$$Z = 0.483 - 0.528 \log Y; \quad \bar{R}^2 = 0.698,$$
$$(9.5) \quad\quad (5.1)$$

where Z is the ratio of imports of goods and nonfactor services to GNP, Y is real GNP in billions of 1974 dollars, and log is the natural logarithm; t-ratios are in parentheses.

FIGURE 3.1   **Relationship of import-GNP ratio to size of economy**

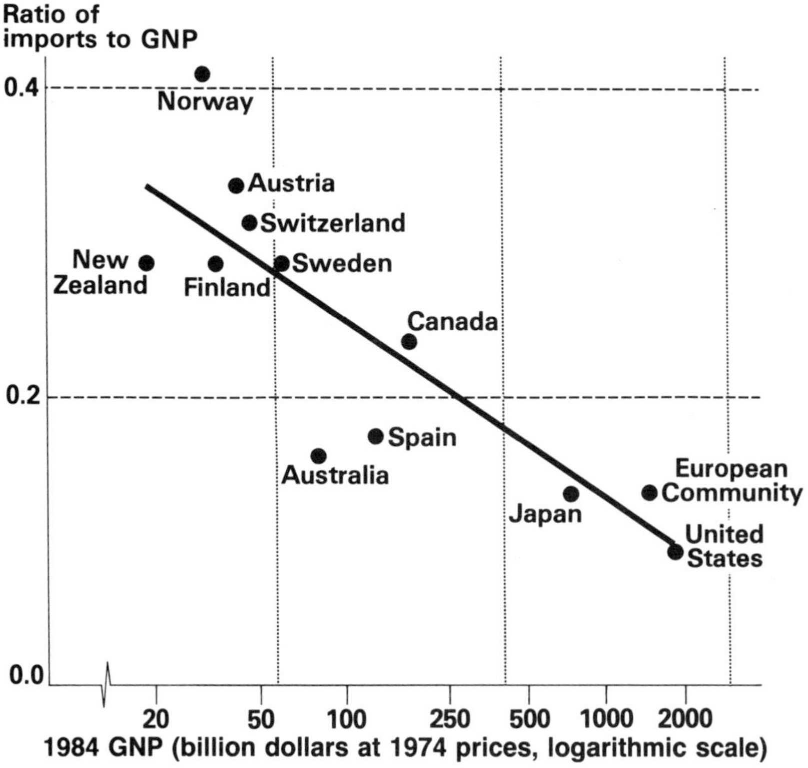

**Ratio of
imports to GNP**

1984 GNP (billion dollars at 1974 prices, logarithmic scale)

Source: Table 3.3.

resources which a country lacks, on the one hand, and the limited domestic absorption of a natural resource the country has in an abundance that permits large exports, on the other, countries with a broadly diversified natural resource base similar to the international average will tend to have a lower ratio of imports to GNP than countries without natural resources or countries with a high concentration of resources in a limited number of raw materials. It is thus desirable to take account of natural resource endowment in international comparisons.

Data on transportation costs are difficult to assemble. However, one indication of their importance is the ratio of the c.i.f. import value (cost including insurance and freight) to their f.o.b. value (free on board). These data do show significantly higher costs for Japan and other Pacific nations than for America and Europe.[34] More direct data on transport costs are available for air cargo. These data also show higher transport costs for the Pacific countries than for the United States and Europe.[35] The statistical tests below use an average of two indexes of transportation costs, corresponding to the c.i.f./f.o.b. measure and the air cargo rates.

Data on natural resources are also sparse. However, they are available for arable land, a measure of agricultural resources. These data show remarkable differences in endowments.[36] Petroleum resources may be represented by annual production of crude oil per capita (by far the highest in Norway, followed by Canada, the United States, and the EEC). The presence of mineral resources may be represented by the existence of significant deposits of iron ore.[37]

These various influences are incorporated into a cross-country test for abnormal protection in Japan, in the following statistical equation:

---

34. Weighting by trade shares in imports from the countries listed in table 3.3, the average excess of c.i.f. over f.o.b. import values in 1974–84 was 10.5 percent for Japan, 9.7 percent for Australia, and 8.9 percent for New Zealand, compared with 5.5 percent for the United States and 5.6 percent for the European Economic Community. Calculated from IMF, *International Financial Statistics*, various issues. Note that these data tend to understate relative transport costs, because they are the ex post result of demand confronted with varying ex ante transport prices, and presumably some volume adjustment of trade away from products with high transport costs leaves the final expense on transportation lower (for high-cost areas) than would be the case in the absence of volume response.

35. Weighted by partner-country shares in imports (for the countries listed in table 3.3), the average cost to ship 100 kilograms by air is $6.13 per kilogram for imports into Japan, $7.96 per kilogram for New Zealand, and $9.81 per kilogram for Australia. In contrast, the average air cargo rate is $3.63 per kilogram for US imports and $3.60 per kilogram for imports into the EEC from nonmember countries. Calculated from *The Air Cargo Tariff*, no. 51, August 1985, general commodity rate. For ocean transport there appears to be no readily available source of comprehensive rate quotations.

36. Japan and Switzerland have the lowest endowments, at 41 and 56 hectares per 1,000 persons. Land endowments are far higher for the United States (876), the EEC (179), and especially Canada (1,736) and Australia (2,944). Calculated from *FAO Production Yearbook 1976*, vol. 30 (Rome, 1977), pp. 45–55, and IMF, *International Financial Statistics Yearbook 1984*.

37. International Energy Agency, "Oil and Gas Statistics," second quarter (OECD, 1984), and Bureau of Mines, Department of the Interior, *Mineral Facts and Problems* (Washington, 1985), p. 4.

(1) $Z = 0.7731 - 0.0628 \log Y + 0.0100 \log P - 0.0378 \log L$
      (28.4)   (26.2)   (7.57)   (7.25)

      $+ 0.0414 I - 0.00069 T + 0.0082 D_J;$ $\bar{R}^2 = 0.8950,$
      (3.96)   (9.7)   (0.47)

where Z is the ratio of imports of goods and nonfactor services to GNP, Y is GNP in real terms at 1974 dollars, as adjusted for cross-country purchasing power differences, P is crude oil production per capita, L is arable land per capita, I is a dummy variable for presence of significant iron ore reserves (1 if present, zero if not), T is the index of transportation costs discussed above, D_J is a dummy variable for Japan (1 for Japan, zero otherwise), and log is the natural logarithm; t-statistics are in parentheses.

This equation is from annual data for 1974 through 1984, for the pool of 11 countries plus the EEC (table 3.3), giving 132 observations. The statistical fit is high (90 percent of variation is successfully explained). All of the economic variables are highly significant in statistical terms (t-statistics well above the level of approximately 2.0 necessary for significance at the 5 percent level). Only one variable is not statistically significant: the dummy variable for Japanese protection. (Even the sign on this variable does not indicate abnormal protection but higher than average imports. However, this coefficient is very small and, being insignificant statistically, should be regarded as zero.)

The estimates for each variable are intuitively plausible. As shown in figure 3.1, there is a negative relationship between the import ratio and the logarithm of GNP, confirmed in the equation. The positive coefficient on oil reflects high imports, especially by Norway, based on high oil exports. The positive coefficient for iron ore deposits indicates a similar process of specialization, exportation, and importation of other goods in countries with abundant iron ore. In contrast, the land coefficient is negative, indicating that countries with more abundant land tend to be more self-sufficient in a variety of agricultural products, while Japan and other land-scarce countries tend to import more than they would otherwise.[38] Finally, the negative coefficient on transport cost confirms the view that higher relative transport expense leads to a relatively lower ratio of imports to GNP.[39]

---

38. An alternative specification of the equation stating the natural resource variables as deviations from cross-country means eliminates the statistical significance of these variables.

39. Note that the statistical results (especially t-statistic) of the level specification of the transport cost index (used in equation 1) are superior to results using a logarithmic specification.

The cross-country statistical test confirms the simple scatter diagram: Japan is basically on the line for international norms of imports relative to GNP, after taking account of natural resource endowment and transportation costs as well as country size. These results suggest that there is nothing special about Japan's import-GNP ratio to attribute to an unusual degree of protection.

An alternative indirect measure of Japan's protection might be the trend in its ratio of imports to GNP over time, in comparison with the corresponding trend in other major countries. One expert has cited a decline in Japan's ratio of imports to GNP from 14.2 percent in Japan's fiscal year 1973 to 13.1 percent in 1983 "in spite of the 44 market-opening measures" as evidence of "the relatively closed market in Japan."[40]

However, Japan's trend in the import-GNP ratio is not much different from that for Canada and the EEC. Table 3.4 shows the import-GNP ratio for these economies and the United States over the last 15 years. (Once again, EEC imports exclude trade among members.) The trend for Japan is intermediate between that for Europe and that for Canada. From 1970–74 to 1980–84, the ratio of imports to GNP rose from an average of 19 percent to 22 percent in Canada, from 9.4 percent to 12.3 percent in the EEC, and from 9.7 percent to 12.1 percent in Japan. The proportionate increase for Japan (one-fourth) was between that for the EEC (one-third) and that for Canada (one-sixth).

It is the United States that stands out as atypical. The US ratio of imports to GNP rose from an average of 5.4 percent in 1970–74 to 9.0 percent in 1980–84, a proportionate increase of two-thirds. In 1980, a high import ratio was associated with the second oil shock. But while the import-GNP ratio moderated from its 1980 high in Japan (just as it did after the first oil shock in 1974), dollar overvaluation kept the US import ratio high in 1981–84.[41]

Measurement of the ratio of *real* imports to *real* GNP, both in constant

---

40. Lawrence B. Krause, statement before the US House of Representatives, Subcommittee on International Economic Policy and Trade, Hearings on US-Japan Trade Relations, 9 May 1985.
41. Faster adjustment to oil prices in Japan accounts for some of the difference. In the mid-1970s, US oil price controls and declining domestic oil production caused a sharp rise in oil imports. Thus, whereas Japan reduced the physical volume of oil imports by 14 percent from 1972 to 1976, the volume of oil imports into the United States rose by 31 percent over this period. Subsequent price liberalization improved US adjustment. By 1983, the physical volume of US imports for the United States had declined to 93 percent of its 1972 level (still a smaller adjustment than in Japan, where the level stood at 66 percent of its 1972 base). Calculated from IMF, *International Financial Statistics Yearbook 1984*, pp. 131, 365, and 595.

TABLE 3.4   **Ratio of imports[a] to GNP, four major trading areas, 1970–84 (percentage)**

Year	United States	Canada	European Economic Community[b]	Japan
1970	4.3	17.1	9.0	9.3
1971	4.5	17.4	8.8	8.6
1972	5.0	18.6	8.6	7.8
1973	5.6	19.7	9.1	9.3
1974	7.7	22.5	11.4	13.5
1975	6.8	21.9	10.7	11.6
1976	7.7	20.4	10.9	11.6
1977	8.4	20.9	11.2	10.4
1978	8.6	22.3	10.8	8.3
1979	9.2	24.6	10.4	11.1
1980	9.8	24.1	10.7	13.6
1981	9.2	24.0	12.2	12.5
1982	8.3	19.5	12.2	12.3
1983	8.2	20.0	12.2	10.9
1984	9.3	23.1	14.0	11.0

Source: IMF, Direction of Trade Statistics, various issues; OECD, Monthly Statistics of Foreign Trade, April 1985; OECD, National Accounts: Main Aggregates, Volume I, 1960–1983; IMF, International Financial Statistics, May 1985.
a. C.i.f.
b. Imports from nonmember countries.

prices, shows a lower trend over time for Japan than for the United States, Canada, and the EEC. Defining 1970–74 as an index base of 100, this ratio of import volume to real GNP by 1980–84 had risen to an index of 119.2 for the EEC, 109.8 for the United States, and 105.7 for Canada, but had fallen to 87.3 for Japan.[42]

---

42. Calculated from IMF, International Financial Statistics Yearbook 1984 and International Financial Statistics, May 1985; and OECD, National Accounts: Main Aggregates, Volume I, 1960–1983, pp. 118–19.

However, nominal ratios of imports to GNP are probably more appropriate for a test of the trend in the economy's openness over time. It is the economic opportunity cost, including effects of price movements, that more accurately reflects the economic significance of imports rather than physical tons or barrels; and because the denominator of the nominal import-GNP ratio also reflects price movements, the effect of general inflation is already neutralized. Indeed, unless the ratio of nominal imports to nominal GNP is used, rather than the real ratio, the measure will fail to register important movements in the terms of trade.

In particular, the proportionate impact of the two oil shocks was greatest on Japan[43] and the corresponding rise in nominal oil imports meant greater pressure to economize on other imports, slowing the real volume growth of imports in purely physical terms. Yoshitomi has analyzed the divergence between the growth of Japan's trade in nominal and real terms.[44] He notes that, from 1972 to 1980, real exports of goods and services grew at 11.6 percent annually, while real imports grew only by 2.2 percent—less than the 4.0 percent real growth rate of GNP. Yet there was an extremely small cumulative current account surplus, because the sharp rise in exports went to pay for the rise in oil prices. Higher oil prices in the period 1972–82 caused a deterioration of 43.3 percent in Japan's terms of trade, equivalent to a real income loss of 10 percent of GNP. Yoshitomi notes that "it is no wonder" that the rapid growth of real exports to pay for higher oil costs "caused trade conflicts between Japan and its partner countries." The same forces contributed to slow growth in real imports relative to GNP.

MANUFACTURED IMPORTS

Some observers argue that Japan's protection may be seen in its low share of manufactures in total imports. The composition of Japan's imports is much more heavily oriented toward primary products than is the case for other major countries. In 1983, manufactured goods accounted for only 22.2

---

43. In 1980, net trade in crude and refined oil and natural gas amounted to a deficit equal to 30.9 percent of imports for the United States and 27.1 percent of imports from nonmembers for the EEC (and a surplus equal to 2 percent of imports for Canada). For Japan, this trade amounted to a deficit equal to 46.1 percent of imports. Calculated from OECD, *Trade by Commodities*, series C, January–December 1980, and IMF, *International Financial Statistics Yearbook 1984*.

44. Masaru Yoshitomi, *Japan as Capital Exporter and the World Economy*, Occasional Paper No. 18 (New York: Group of Thirty, 1985), pp. 6–7.

percent of Japan's imports, compared with 61.2 percent for the United States, 78.9 percent for Canada, and 55.8 percent for imports into the EEC as a bloc.[45]

Heavy concentration of imports in primary goods (including food and oil) is, however, primarily a reflection of Japan's limited endowment of natural resources. The composition of the country's *exports* reveals this fact vividly. Only 4.2 percent of Japan's exports are in primary products, while 95.8 percent are in manufactures. In contrast, primary products account for 32.9 percent of US exports and 45.2 percent of Canada's exports. Even the EEC obtains 27.5 percent of its exports from primary products.[46]

These data indicate that Japan's comparative advantage is much more sharply oriented toward manufactures, and away from raw materials, than is the case for any other major industrial trading area. This pattern of comparative advantage is not surprising given Japan's limited natural resources. Japan's extremely low ratio of arable land to population has been noted above. Similarly, the United States, Canada, and the EEC have domestic oil (and other energy) reserves while Japan has practically none.

Nowhere are the implications of natural resource scarcity for Japan's concentration in manufactured exports and raw materials imports more forceful than in the area of energy. The two oil price shocks of the past decade have pushed Japan into an even greater reliance on manufactured exports to pay for raw material imports. As just noted, Japan's terms of trade declined by 43.3 percent from 1972 to 1982 due to the increased price of oil—requiring a sharp increase in manufactured exports, since that is virtually the only category that Japan *can* sell abroad, and a cutback in nonoil imports (including manufactures) to pay the higher oil bill. The US Council of Economic Advisers has attributed Japan's large surpluses in manufactures trade, and in bilateral US-Japan trade, to the "huge deficits in its trade in primary products, especially oil, and with primary producers, especially the Organization of Petroleum Exporting Countries (OPEC)."[47]

---

45. GATT, *International Trade 1983/84* (Geneva, 1984), tables A23–A26. The GATT definition of manufactures excludes copper and processed foods.

46. *Ibid.*

47. Council of Economic Advisers, *Economic Report of the President 1985* (Washington, February 1985), p. 56. The authors note that "Japan does maintain restrictions which seriously hurt US businesses. . . . [But] these trade restrictions probably do not lead to a larger overall Japanese trade surplus. If they were removed, the yen would depreciate and increased imports in the currently protected sectors would be offset by reduced deficits or increased surpluses elsewhere."

The Office of the US Trade Representative has proposed an imaginative methodology to determine whether Japan imports a reasonable amount of manufactured goods after adjusting for the country's lack of comparative advantage in natural resources. This approach considers natural resource imports as a percentage of GNP for the United States as a benchmark. It then asks what would happen if Japan's ratio of natural resource imports to GNP were no higher than the US benchmark. The resulting savings on resource imports would permit the yen to appreciate, according to the USTR analysis. As a result, Japan's exports would decline and its manufactured imports would rise until a new equilibrium was established (with the same trade balance as before).

Division of the adjustment between reduced exports and increased manufactured imports is allocated according to econometric estimates of the price elasticity of foreign demand for Japan's exports and Japan's price elasticity of demand for manufactured imports. The USTR analysis finds that, from an actual level of 2.9 percent of GDP for Japan's manufactured imports in 1983, adjustment for resource endowment following this methodology boosts manufactured imports only to 3.3 percent of GDP. By contrast, US manufactured imports were 5.0 percent of GDP in 1983. The USTR analysis concludes that only a small portion of the shortfall in Japan's ratio of manufactured imports to GDP can be explained by its poor endowment of natural resources, and that accordingly, the low level of manufactured imports is primarily evidence of protection.[48]

The USTR method makes no correction for the fact that US imports in 1983 were bloated by exchange rate overvaluation. Neither does it take account of higher transportation costs for Japan. In addition, the methodology appears biased toward the conclusion that Japan's imports are abnormally low.[49] Hence, we would continue to conclude that Japan's limited endowment

---

48. Office of the US Trade Representative, "US Statement on Japanese Market Access."

49. Consider two countries that have identical ratios of total imports to GDP (and the same GDP). The one with the lower share of natural resource imports (country U) is taken as the benchmark. The "adjustment" for the other country (J) reduces its resource imports to the (lower) benchmark of the first country (U). Unless the price elasticity of foreign demand for country J's exports is zero, the next step in the USTR methodology will necessarily raise the hypothetical level of J's manufactured imports by *less* than it has reduced the level of its natural resource imports. The conclusion of this approach will inevitably be that country J has a lower *total* import-GDP ratio, *and* a lower ratio of manufactured imports to GDP, than country U

of natural resources is the primary explanation for the lower share of manufactured goods in its total imports.

Other analysts have argued that Japan would have higher manufacturing imports if its market were less protected because of the process of intra-industry trade. In this process, two-way trade flows may occur even within a given industry as firms take advantage of specialization and economies of scale on individual product lines. Japan's intra-industry trade is much lower than that of the United States and major European countries.[50]

Balassa has carried out statistical tests relating intra-industry trade to underlying economic variables.[51] On the basis of theoretical work in recent years, intra-industry trade would be expected to be higher in countries with higher per capita income (because their trade tends to be more in products "differentiated" by taste—such as automobiles—than in homogeneous goods), larger domestic economies (which permit specialization through economies of scale), and lower transportation costs; and among bordering countries and members of free-trade areas. Balassa's statistical tests for 38 countries confirm these influences, and find that Japan is almost exactly on the cross-country line of predicted intra-industry specialization.[52] Japan's intra-industry trade is lower than that of almost all of the other industrial countries (except for Australia), but higher than that of most developing countries.

Considering that large economic size and high per capita income would lead to a high incidence of intra-industry trade, transportation cost is apparently

---

after adjustment for natural resources. The diagnosis of protection follows automatically from the methodology.

It might be argued in reply that one should expect the total import-GDP ratio of resource-poor country J to be *higher* than that of country U, so that, in the absence of protection, adjustment of resource imports to the country U benchmark would raise country J's manufactured imports just enough that after adjustment the ratios of manufactured imports and total imports to GDP were identical to those of country U. However, insofar as natural resource endowment is a factor, the cross-country statistical test reported above finds that even after taking account of the influence of natural resources, Japan's total import-GNP ratio is at the level that would be expected from international patterns, rather than below that level as implied by the USTR analysis.

50. See, for example, Scott, "US Competitiveness," p. 37. Scott emphasizes that Japan's intra-industry trade is also lower than that of Korea, Taiwan, Hong Kong, and Singapore and concludes that lack of natural resources cannot justify Japan's low degree of intra-industry trade.

51. Bela Balassa, "Intra-Industry Specialization: A Multi-Country Perspective," World Bank Discussion Paper No. DRD82 (Washington, June 1984).

52. *Ibid.*, figure 1.

the main influence explaining low intra-industry trade in Japan. These transportation costs would be expected to be lower for intra-industry trade between Japan and the East Asian newly industrializing countries (NICs). And indeed, Japanese intra-industry trade with these countries has grown rapidly in recent years and, for sectors in which such trade would be expected, it stands at relatively high levels.[53]

The relationship between the ratio of imports to GNP and the share of manufactures in imports, as alternative tests of protection, also requires clarification. Some observers argue that protection need not reduce the ratio of imports to GNP but only alter the composition of imports. The implication is that the low level of manufactures in Japan's imports is a better guide to the presence of high protection than the ratio of total imports to GNP.

However, this proposition is incorrect. At the theoretical level, protection does reduce the ratio of total imports to GNP. Protection raises the price of import substitutes relative to exports. In response, resources shift out of exports, and the country earns less total foreign exchange than under free trade. With fixed international prices, less foreign exchange means lower total imports (for the small country; in a large country that can depress world prices by cutting its demand for foreign goods, protection would reduce the import-GNP ratio even further). At the level of actual experience, the plummeting ratio of imports to GNP in major countries during the 1930s as protective barriers mounted, and the sharp drop in the ratio of imports to GNP in Latin America in the 1950s and 1960s as countries pursued high protection for import-substituting industrialization, provide ample evidence that high protection reduces the ratio of imports to GNP in addition to altering the product composition of imports.

Additional insight into the issue of Japan's manufactured, as opposed to total, imports may be obtained through a consideration of actual US manufactured exports to Japan in comparison with those to other major markets. Japan is the second largest national market (after Canada) for US manufactured exports (table 3.5), consistent with its second-place ranking by size of total national imports. (The exceptionally high level of Canada's imports of manufactures from the United States is explained by geographical propinquity, as is the similarly disproportionate rank of Mexico; table 3.5.) Thus, Japan is already the second most valuable customer for US exports of manufactures.

---

53. Yoko Sazanami, ''Possibilities of Expanding Intra-Industry Trade in Japan,'' *Keio Economic Studies*, vol. 18, no. 2, 1981.

T A B L E   3.5   **US exports of manufactures[a] to major markets, 1983 (million dollars and rankings)**

Country	US manufactured exports	Rank	Total country imports	Rank
Canada	30,802	1	65,059	6
Japan	10,219	2	126,437	2
United Kingdom	8,415	3	100,071	4
Mexico	6,182	4	11,267	19
Germany	5,939	5	152,941	1
Saudi Arabia	5,916	6	39,198	9
France	4,673	7	105,416	3
Netherlands	3,930	8	62,562	7
Australia	3,506	9	21,461	16
South Korea	3,079	10	26,192	13
Belgium	3,047	11	55,317	8
Singapore	2,996	12	28,158	12
Taiwan	2,477	13	20,287	17
Italy	2,170	14	80,362	5
Switzerland	2,047	15	29,192	11
Venezuela	1,856	16	8,710	20
Hong Kong	1,838	17	24,013	15
Brazil	1,731	18	16,801	18
Sweden	1,210	19	26,097	14
Spain	1,134	20	29,193	10

Source: OECD, *Foreign Trade by Commodities, Volume I: Exports,* series C, 1983 (1985); and IMF, *International Financial Statistics,* May 1985.
a.   Standard International Trade Classification (SITC) sectors 5 through 9.

Table 3.6 sheds additional light on the issue of manufactured exports. The table shows US exports in 1983 of manufactures to the three largest national markets—Canada, Japan, and Germany—with detail by principal categories. One-third of US manufactured exports to Canada are accounted for by the special case of road vehicles, in which North American production is fully integrated. Among the other detailed categories, it is informative to consider sectors often believed to be highly protected (overtly or indirectly) in Japan.

TABLE 3.6   **US manufactured exports to Canada, Japan, and Germany, by category, 1983 (million dollars)**

SITC Number	Product	Canada	Japan	Germany
5–9	Manufactures, total	30,802	10,219	5,939
5	Chemical products	2,537	2,613	901
54	Pharmaceuticals	192	527	160
6	Manufactures classified by material	3,994	1,386	547
61	Leather	67	16	10
63	Cork and wood	101	22	73
64	Paper, paperboard	489	293	86
7	Machinery and transport equipment	20,653	4,780	3,567
71	Power generating	2,360	520	286
75	Office machines	1,555	900	1,113
76	Telecommunications	438	208	194
77	Electrical machinery	1,715	723	598
78	Road vehicles	10,092	141	226
8	Miscellaneous manufactures	2,648	1,359	850
	Memorandum item			
	Imports from all sources	65,059	126,437	152,941 (82,242)[a]
	Manufactured imports from United States as percentage of total imports	47.3 (37.7)[b]	8.1	3.9 (7.2)[a]

Source: See table 3.5.
a. Excluding imports from the European Economic Community.
b. Excluding road vehicles.

In pharmaceuticals, US exports to Japan are much higher than to Canada and Germany. In telecommunications, US exports to Japan exceed those to Germany, and the same is true of paper and paperboard and electrical machinery.

US exports of office machinery are modestly lower to Japan than to

Germany, a possible indication of import impediments. The only sector that seems to show a very substantial shortfall of Japan's imports, compared with those of Canada and Germany, is wood products, where high Japanese tariffs on plywood clearly do represent a problem.

Overall, table 3.6 provides little support for the hypothesis that US manufactured exports to Japan are abnormally low even in the sectors often cited as highly protected. This evidence is all the more significant considering that Germany is widely regarded as having one of the least protected markets among the industrial countries. Neither does consideration of the special factor of Germany's trade with the EEC reverse the implication that US manufactured exports to Japan are at least comparable to those to Germany. As shown in table 3.6, even if Germany's imports from the EEC are excluded, the ratio of Germany's imports of manufactures from the United States to its (non-EEC) total imports is still somewhat smaller (7.2 percent) than the ratio of Japan's imports of US manufactures to Japan's total imports (8.1 percent). And if the comparison is made on a basis including EEC supply, Germany's purchases of US manufactures are only half as large in relative terms (3.9 percent of total imports) as Japan's (8.1 percent).

A final aspect of manufactured imports concerns those from the NICs and other developing countries. The USTR and others have specifically criticized Japan for absorbing less than its fair share of imports of manufactures from developing countries.[54]

Balassa has calculated that, from 1973 to 1981, the share of manufactured imports from developing countries in domestic consumption of manufactured goods ("import-penetration ratio") rose from 1.1 percent to 2.3 percent in the United States and from 0.9 percent to 2.0 percent in the EEC, but only from 0.7 percent to 1.0 percent in Japan.[55] Both the lower level and the slower increase for Japan might suggest greater protection in Japan than in the other major industrial countries, against manufactured goods from developing countries.

With regard to the level of import penetration, however, the product definition for manufactures used by Balassa (as well as GATT) excludes a range of manufactured exports that are important for developing countries.

---

54. Office of the USTR, US Statement on Japanese Market Access, p. 11.

55. Bela Balassa, *Trends in International Trade in Manufactured Goods and Structural Change in the Industrial Countries,* World Bank Staff Working Paper No. 611, Washington, 1984, p. 11.

Standard International Trade Classification (SITC) classes 5 through 8, less 68, exclude copper as well as processed foods. Using a broader definition based on the International Standard Industrial Classification (ISIC, categories 311 to 390, excluding 353—petroleum refineries), Cline has calculated elsewhere that in 1978 the import-penetration ratio for developing-country supply in manufactured goods was 2.28 percent in the United States, 2.50 percent in Japan, and an average of 2.10 for Germany, France, Italy, and the United Kingdom.[56] On this basis, Japan's imports of manufactures from developing countries were actually somewhat higher (in relative terms) than those of the United States and Europe.

The difference in the two data sets is meaningful in economic terms. The sectors excluded in the narrower definition of manufactures (copper, preserved fruits and vegetables, canned fish, agricultural oils, processed grains, sugar, confectionery, other processed foods, and tobacco products) tend to be precisely the natural-resource-based manufactures in which Japan has a comparative disadvantage and therefore tends to import relatively more.

With respect to the trend over time, there is an important reason to expect that Japan's import-penetration ratio for manufactured goods from developing countries would have risen less rapidly than those for the United States and Europe. As analyzed above, the two oil shocks have intensified Japan's need to specialize in manufactured exports, relative to the United States and Europe. One would then expect that, in 1973–81, Japan's import-penetration ratio in manufactures (including those from developing countries) would have grown more slowly than those of the United States and Europe.

In sum, neither the level nor the trend in import penetration for manufactured goods from developing countries suggests higher protection in Japan than in Europe and the United States.

Indirect evidence on Japan's protection through cross-country comparisons is available at the microeconomic level as well as the level of national

---

56. Cline, *Exports of Manufactures from Developing Countries*, p. 14. For comparison, Balassa's estimates for 1978 using the narrower definition are: United States, 1.8 percent; EEC, 1.6 percent; and Japan, 0.8 percent. Balassa, *Trends in International Trade*, p. 11. Unpublished calculations by Balassa show that the US ratio had risen to 3.1 percent by 1983 while Japan's remained at 1 percent. However, the 1983 level for the United States is distorted by dollar overvaluation. Using Cline's estimates, the difference in trend is much less pronounced. From 1970 to 1978 the US penetration ratio rose from 1.05 to 2.28; the ratio for Japan, from 1.90 to 2.50; and for the four largest European countries, from an average of 1.70 to 2.10, giving a somewhat larger proportionate rise in Japan than in Europe.

aggregates. Gary R. Saxonhouse has estimated statistical equations explaining net trade (exports *minus* imports) in 109 specific product sectors over the period 1959–73.[57] For each of nine countries, these equations relate net trade to endowments of productive resources: capital stock, labor, educational attainment (human capital), petroleum resources, iron ore resources, and arable land.[58] In addition, "distance" is an explanatory variable of each country's net trade in the commodity, measured as the average number of miles of each country from its major trading partners, weighted by the share of trade with each.

Essentially, Saxonhouse's model is a detailed statistical application of the theory of comparative advantage. Countries with relatively high endowments of land, for example, should tend to have high net exports of agricultural commodities. Countries with relatively high endowments of unskilled labor would be expected to have high net exports in labor-intensive products. Beyond these economic variables, Saxonhouse incorporates country-specific (dummy) variables. If a country is unusually protective in a particular commodity, its country-specific term will show lower imports (higher net exports) than can be explained by factors of production alone.

The results of these tests do not show Japan as more protective than other major trading nations. Only 17 of 109 sectors, accounting for 4.9 percent of Japan's trade, indicate a significant protective differential for Japan. Only one of these sectors—"saw logs and veneer logs"—is among the sectors under current controversy in US-Japanese trade. In contrast, significant protective departures are found for 24 sectors in Italy (11.7 percent of trade), 32 in France (16.0 percent), and 43 in Korea (28.3 percent of trade).

The Saxonhouse study thus supports at the microeconomic level the general findings presented here at the aggregate level: on the basis of cross-country comparisons there is little evidence that Japan is more protective than other major trading nations. The results found by Saxonhouse may be open to criticism, however, because Japan's physical distance from markets is so great that the distance variable may be picking up what would otherwise be attributed to Japanese protection (although the presence of Korea in the estimates reduces this likelihood, and the country-specific terms for Korea do pick up substantial incidence of protection). Reformulation of the distance

---

57. Saxonhouse, "The Micro- and Macroeconomics of Foreign Sales to Japan," pp. 259–304.
58. The countries are: Canada, France, Germany, Italy, Japan, Korea, the Netherlands, the United Kingdom, and the United States.

variable in terms of actual transport costs by commodity would help remove any bias from this source. Also, the country-specific terms do not vary over time, and it would seem likely that Japan's relative level of protection was considerably higher in the 1960s than in the 1970s and early 1980s. (Note, however, that the Saxonhouse method allows for this fact indirectly insofar as countries at lower stages of development have higher protection.) Nonetheless, the Saxonhouse study is an important piece of empirical, microeconomic research that tends to cast doubt on the proposition that Japan is substantially more protective than other major trading countries.

COMPLAINTS BY OTHER COUNTRIES

US exporters are not alone in complaining about Japanese protection. As noted above, European complaints reached the level of an unusual submission to GATT, charging that the entire Japanese economic system discriminated against imports. Korean exporters of steel and other products also reportedly find it difficult to penetrate the Japanese market.

However, it is even clearer in the case of other countries than in the case of the United States that, whatever the base level of Japan's protection, there is no evidence of a deterioration in trade balance in recent years caused by intensified protection in Japan. Table 3.7 presents Japan's bilateral trade balance in 1980 and 1984 with the large trading countries reviewed in chapter 1. In absolute terms, Japan's trade balance increased with respect to only 8 of 23 major trading partners, and decreased with respect to the other 15. Relative to the base of bilateral trade (turnover), Japan's trade balance increased with 9 countries and decreased with 14. Only Canada showed a proportionate increase in the bilateral deficit with Japan comparable to that of the United States (25 percent of trade turnover).

In an important dimension, then, Japan's trade performance relative to the United States is atypical of its performance relative to other countries. It is inaccurate to view the surging US bilateral deficit with Japan as merely part of a common pattern whereby all other major countries also have experienced similar sharp bilateral deteriorations with Japan. Instead, it is the United States that stands alone in extreme erosion of its bilateral trade balance with Japan in the early 1980s.

TABLE 3.7   **Japan's bilateral trade balance[a] with major trading countries, 1980 and 1984 (million dollars and ratios)**

Country	Trade balance		As fraction of bilateral turnover[b]		
	1980	1984	1980	1984	1980–84 change
Argentina	714	−98	0.55	−0.11	−0.66
Australia	−3,611	−2,105	−0.35	−0.17	0.18
Austria	231	227	0.40	0.37	−0.04
Belgium	1,056	879	0.58	0.48	−0.10
Brazil	−451	−1,351	−0.17	−0.52	−0.35
Canada	−2,303	−641	−0.32	−0.07	0.25
Denmark	109	46	0.14	0.03	−0.12
France	726	701	0.22	0.22	0.00
Germany	3,282	3,930	0.40	0.42	0.03
Hong Kong	4,211	5,707	0.79	0.77	−0.01
Italy	17	−15	0.01	−0.06	−0.02
Korea	2,353	3,006	0.28	0.26	−0.02
Mexico	289	−1,369	0.13	−0.44	−0.57
Netherlands	1,688	1,378	0.69	0.61	−0.08
Norway	313	199	0.46	0.25	−0.21
China, P.R.	763	1,256	0.08	0.10	0.02
Romania	136	−60	0.50	−0.30	−0.80
Singapore	2,413	2,829	0.44	0.44	0.00
Spain	272	224	0.26	0.21	−0.05
Sweden	331	537	0.26	0.36	0.10
Switzerland	95	−871	0.04	−0.29	−0.33
United Kingdom	1,841	2,404	0.32	0.35	0.03
United States	7,343	33,542	0.13	0.38	0.25

Source: IMF, *Direction of Trade Statistics Yearbook 1985*, pp. 241–42.

a. Japan's exports, f.o.b., minus its imports, c.i.f.

b. Trade turnover = exports plus imports.

SUMMARY

Indirect evidence of intangible protection is complicated both in conceptual terms and in empirical demonstration. We would rely primarily on the ratio of total imports to GNP. Cross-country comparisons of this ratio suggest that Japan shows no special aberration of low imports that might be attributable to high but intangible protection, after taking account of country size, natural resource endowment, and transportation costs. And although the share of manufactures in Japan's total imports is low, there are sound reasons of comparative advantage to expect this pattern. Moreover, Japan is the second largest market for US exports of manufactures; US manufactured exports to Japan compare favorably with those to Germany, even though Germany is generally considered to have a relatively unprotected market. One important study at the level of individual products also appears to confirm the macroeconomic evidence that Japanese protection is not abnormally high.

Institutional Evidence

The indirect evidence on protection considered above is primarily macro-quantitative. However, the image of Japan as a protected country derives primarily from descriptive material that is microqualitative, usually in the form of examples from the experiences of businessmen who have found it difficult to penetrate the Japanese market. Most of this evidence may be called anecdotal, in the sense that it is undocumented except by word of mouth (often from a single unconfirmed source). There is also a limited body of case history analysis by scholars (and by affected industry groups) describing Japanese protection. This section reviews both types of institutional evidence.

It is important to recognize that there is no assurance that the examples noted here are representative. It would require a statistically valid sample of US businesses attempting to export to Japan to determine whether the repertoire of protection anecdotes is representative. Indeed, a 1982 sample survey of the American business community in Japan, conducted by the American Chamber of Commerce in Japan, found only a minority of responses indicating protective barriers.[59] Another survey of US businessmen working

---

59. American Chamber of Commerce in Japan, "Report on 1981/82 Trade-Investment Barrier Membership Survey" (Tokyo, 8 March 1982; processed), and "US-Japan Trade and Investment," ACCJ Position Papers (prepared for presentation in Washington, 18–22 May 1982; processed).

in Japan, conducted by Arthur D. Little, Inc., found that half of those surveyed believed that bureaucratic and other intentional discrimination against foreign products had been eliminated.[60]

However, seminars held at the Institute for International Economics in 1982–84 and extensive discussions with US officials and businessmen have generated a number of anecdotes on Japanese protection. We cite them here without taking responsibility for their accuracy, because they are not readily verifiable. Nonetheless, the body of anecdotes takes on a policy significance because, as the same cases are frequently repeated, they form an important part of the informational background affecting the attitudes of policymakers:

• A representative of a large US electronics corporation stated that it is only possible to sell prototypes of high tech products to Japan, and then only if the technical drawings are included.

• A frequently repeated report is that Korean steel exporters are able to obtain their modest market share in Japan only by delivering the steel surreptitiously, usually at night under tarpaulins and with Korean identification effaced.

• A recently reported incident concerns a small Japanese gasoline distributor that wanted to import from Singapore. Japanese policy reportedly keeps domestically refined heating oil cheap and gasoline expensive to the public. Although there is no legal impediment to imports, pressure by Japanese refiners and distributors reportedly forced the company to sell its inventory of the gasoline to a Japanese refining company and discontinue imports.

• A former official of a Japanese semiconductor company informed a US negotiator that Japanese firms buy chips first from within their own company, second from a company within their group, third from other Japanese companies, and last from abroad.

• Honda and Sony are reported to have invested abroad because of the difficulty of breaking into the domestic Japanese market held by major keiretsu.

• Acrylo nitrile for synthetic fibers is reportedly 30 percent more expensive

---

60. Arthur D. Little, Inc., *The Japanese Non-Tariff Trade Barrier Issue: American Views and Implications for Japan-US Trade Relations* (Cambridge, Mass., 1979).

in Japan than the US export price. Imports are controlled by a few trading companies, which are shareholders in competing Japanese petroleum firms.

• Until recently, soda ash imports were protected by a cartel that controlled unloading facilities. Each of five US manufacturers was allowed to bring in only one boatload annually by each of five corresponding trading companies.

• Trading companies are unwilling to import fertilizer because they consider it politically unwise.

• A recent Nissan purchase of the super-computer produced by the American firm Cray came only after pressure from US negotiators. Otherwise, Nissan would have bought from Hitachi, a member of its keiretsu group.

• A representative of one of the largest Japanese automobile companies reportedly stated that the firm always purchases computers from the leading Japanese firm (not including IBM-Japan) because that company reciprocates and buys cars from the auto company.

• Most of the blood plasma in Japan comes from the United States, but only Japanese firms are able to import it.

If the thrust of this oral tradition is unvarnished protection, the message of case history analysis is both more subtle and deeper in its implications. This institutional literature tends to emphasize that protection in Japan is only one facet of a more important phenomenon: what Chalmers Johnson calls the "developmental state."[61] Broadly, that literature emphasizes that Japan engages in planned economic growth with flexible cooperation between the state and the private sector, and that protection of "infant industries" in some form often results until these industries are internationally competitive and can penetrate world export markets.

Johnson notes that Japan's infant industry protection has shifted over the years. Until the early 1960s, the government allocated foreign exchange. By the late 1960s, these controls were removed, yet the authorities felt threatened

---

61. Chalmers Johnson, *MITI and the Japanese Miracle: The Growth of Industrial Policy, 1925–1975* (Stanford, Calif.: Stanford University Press, 1982). This study and the other case-history study discussed below (Vogel, note 64) find a greater role for government intervention and protection than some alternative analyses, however. See the discussion of industrial targeting above, as well as Gary R. Saxonhouse, "What Is All This About 'Industrial Targeting' in Japan?", and Philip H. Trezise, "Industrial Policy in Japan," in Margaret E. Dewer, ed., *Industrial Vitalization: Toward a National Industrial Policy* (New York: Pergamon Press, 1982), pp. 177–95.

by foreign investment takeover under the capital liberalization commitments undertaken in entering into the Organization for Economic Cooperation and Development (OECD) in 1964. The Ministry of International Trade and Industry (MITI) responded with rules that effectively limited foreign investment except for marginal industries, while at the same time pushing domestic mergers to achieve large firms with economies of scale to match foreign competition (such as New Japan Steel, the world's largest steel company, formed in 1970). The strategy sometimes backfired because of independent-minded domestic firms; Mitsubishi shocked MITI by forming a partnership with Chrysler rather than going along with domestic merger plans.[62]

With its role revitalized by the challenge of the oil shock, in the 1970s MITI extended its traditional sectoral criteria (high income elasticity, high productivity growth) to new areas (environmental impact, knowledge-intensive) and identified new leading sectors to follow the success of the automobile: computers (already stressed in the late 1960s), semiconductors, numerically controlled machine tools, robots, and advanced consumer electronics (such as video recorders). In the same period, MITI was creating cartels in structurally depressed industries (textiles, rubber, steel, nonferrous metals, shipbuilding) to allocate cutbacks in capacity and employment. Yet "by the mid-1970s MITI realized that protectionism could no longer be used as one of its policy tools."[63] Johnson thus sees state guidance of development and sectoral adjustment as central to the Japanese economy, but he views overt protection as largely absent since the early 1970s and in fact makes little mention of even tacit protection in more recent years.

Vogel has examined in depth four major Japanese sectors: shipbuilding, machine tools and robots, coal mining, and the information complex (including computers and semiconductors).[64] He cites machine tools as a sector not given much special government assistance. However, until the early 1960s, foreign exchange for imports was denied if a domestic machine tool could perform the function. The firm Yamazaki Tekko grew from "rugged entrepreneurial spirit" rather than government favor, and eventually became the largest engine lathe producer in the world.

In numerically controlled machine tools, government was more active.

---

62. *Ibid.*, pp. 25, 276–78, 286.

63. *Ibid.*, p. 303.

64. Ezra Vogel, *Comeback Case by Case: Building the Resurgence of American Business* (New York: Simon and Schuster, 1985).

Fujitsu's subsidiary, FANUC, was making rapid technological progress in the late 1960s and by the early 1970s caught a "complacent" General Electric off-guard. The government helped by mandating that, by 1977, half of the machine tools produced by Japanese firms must be computer numerically controlled (CNC). This large captive market allowed FANUC and other Japanese suppliers to achieve economies of scale. Under capital liberalization in 1970, foreigners could invest in machine tools but not in CNC machine tools. Moreover, imported CNC machine tools were classified as computers and subject to duties higher than on normal machine tools (but only by 10 percent, a figure Vogel omits). Government labs contributed to research, as did funds from the national railway system (a large CNC user). Japan expanded exports of machine tools to the United States from $10 million in 1971 to $600 million in 1980. While Vogel assigns much of the credit for the success to the efforts of FANUC on its own, he also credits "strategic protectionism and cartelization at critical stages. . . ."[65]

Vogel's review of coal indicates the Japanese willingness to phase down a dying industry (with employment in Kyushu coal mining declining from 105,000 in 1961 to 37,000 in 1967) and bring in new sectors to the affected region. This history is largely one without major protection, except for a levy on oil to finance adjustment programs.[66]

In the information industry, Vogel describes a process of government intervention and protection more subtle than traditional barriers.[67] In 1960, IBM-Japan had been allowed entry as a wholly owned subsidiary because of its technological dominance, and until the 1970s domestic firms conceded the mainframe market to it. By 1976 the government had been forced by international pressure to reduce tariffs on computers, but offered domestic companies subsidies to adjust—contingent on their joint cooperation in production and research. A super-high–performance research project from 1972 to 1976 helped domestic firms upgrade to compete with IBM and domestic firms made path-breaking progress in Chinese characters and voice recognition. By 1979 Fujitsu passed IBM in the domestic market, assisted

---

65. *Ibid.*, pp. 70, 73–74, 83, 89; and US General Accounting Office, *United States–Japan Trade: Issues and Problems* (Washington, 1979).

66. *Ibid.*, chapter 5.

67. ". . . In the 1970s, with the new pressures of internationalization, Japan had no choice but to reduce or remove formal tariff barriers . . . The challenge . . . was to find new ways to protect the home market and reduce purchases of (foreign) goods and services in high technology, in which Japan hoped to catch up, until the country became competitive." *Ibid.*, p. 126.

by many Japanese government corporations that bought only domestic machines (excluding IBM-Japan).[68]

The government had also encouraged the semiconductor industry as a first phase to a sophisticated computer industry. In its very large scale integrated circuit (VLSI) project (1976–79), MITI used research grants to firms, insisting on joint research. MITI selected large, vertically integrated firms to keep intermediate purchases within the group.[69] With the VSLI project, Japanese firms were well positioned in 1979 to meet a shortage of I6K-RAM chips in the US market. However, the program concentrated on a strategically important but limited market segment, the 64K RAM, and by 1982 Japanese firms held 70 percent of the world market.[70]

Telecommunications is the third pillar of the information industry. In the United States, the AT&T monopoly and its subsidiary supplier Western Electric had meant minimal imports of telecommunications equipment. In Japan, government-owned NTT similarly purchased from its four "family members." Pressure was building inside Japan (including from MITI) for privatization of NTT because of its high prices, even as the deregulation wave was leading to the breakup of AT&T. In 1980, the United States and Japan formally agreed to open telephone companies in both countries to competitive bids. However, by 1984, NTT's imports were only 3 percent to 4 percent of its purchases, while Japanese firms were able to sell far more telecommunications equipment in the United States. Foreign firms complained that NTT procurement procedures required detailed technical information that helped NTT family members develop while foreign company sales were rarely achieved. In communications satellites, Japan decided to develop its own rocket-launching capacity, and NTT is seeking to delay purchases of foreign satellites until Japan has its own capacity. Vogel concludes: "Now that leaders are committed to free trade, it is difficult to overcome habits and institutions that had come to be taken for granted."[71]

---

68. *Ibid.*, pp. 139, 141, 152.

69. "With vertical integration, even without nontariff barriers, it would be difficult for foreigners to sell semiconductors or other computer parts in the Japanese market. Although Japanese companies in the [VSLI] project did specialize in producing certain kinds of chips and sold specialized chips to one another after the project was over, by the end of the project they bought very few chips from foreign companies." *Ibid.*, p. 144.

70. *Ibid.*, p. 146.

71. *Ibid.*, p. 176.

Consideration of the list of anecdotes and the two institutional studies reviewed here suggests the following conclusions. First, the anecdotes tend to be minor episodes that in themselves probably do not represent major export losses for foreigners. However, the combined effect of such anecdotes does tend to be a poisoning of the atmosphere that not only inflames US legislators but also probably discourages many US businessmen from even attempting to enter the Japanese market. Adverse perception thus serves as an indirect trade barrier, limiting US exports to an incalculable extent. Second, the case histories show a consensus that, under international pressure, Japan had generally phased out formal protection by the mid-1970s. Third, the case histories and the anecdotes together suggest that much of remaining protection is in the private sector in the form of keiretsu behavior (subject to the doubts about such restrictive behavior raised above). The principal vestige of government protection that emerges from these cases is that of government procurement (NTT), and Vogel recognizes that at the top levels the government now pushes an opening to imports.

There are two other inferences from the institutional information (anecdotal and in case histories) that are more disturbing. One is that some highly competitive Japanese industries of today may be the consequence of formal and informal protection and subsidies in the past. To the extent that this pattern exists, it raises the question of current response to past (but discontinued) protection. Is there a statute of limitations on policy response to foreign protection, and should there be? If retaliation is decreed against actions taken a decade earlier, how would it fit into existing international trade rules—and would it set a precedent that could come back to haunt the United States?

Perhaps the most challenging issue raised by the case histories is the problem of infant-industry development. Before the 1970s, Japan used infant-industry protection; subsequently, it used infant-industry research subsidies, economies-of-scale cartels, and probably government procurement discrimination. When Japan was technologically backward and war-impoverished, its infant-industry strategy may have been appropriate in international terms. For a Japan at the technological frontier, however, strategies learned and carried out in a period of underdevelopment may be unacceptable internationally (as is already clear regarding tariffs and overt nontariff barriers).

Insofar as the effect of infant-industry stimulus is primarily technological advance (for example, computerized voice recognition), surely it would be counterproductive for the world as a whole to stifle such efforts. If Japan and other advanced countries pursue infant-industry stimulus in purely domestic sectors, such as the bullet train, that too should be a matter of international indifference or applause. But where the principal effect of infant-industry stimulus is to capture world market shares in existing technology from other leaders, there would seem to be little justification for infant-industry intervention within already mature countries. Instead, this class of infant-industry stimulus is likely to lead to trade conflict and increasing demands for sectoral reciprocity.

Exchange Rate Protection?

A sophisticated version of the attack on Japan as a bastion of trade protection recognizes the centrality of the exchange rate problem and goes on to argue that the Japanese have consistently manipulated, i.e., depressed, the yen in order to maintain an unfair advantage for Japanese firms in world trade. The primary techniques for doing so could include direct intervention in the exchange markets, through sales of yen against dollars or other currencies, and keeping Japanese interest rates low or taking other steps to promote net capital outflow and thus weaken the yen indirectly. The possibility of such "exchange rate protection" or "exchange rate dumping" has begun to be addressed in the trade literature in recent years.

The Japanese case is, as usual, extremely complicated. Japan did not run consistent current account surpluses until the 1980s, and recorded sizable deficits after the two oil shocks (chapter 2). Hence, it is difficult to detect any persistent tendency to yen undervaluation which has produced overall external surpluses. As recently as 1978, the yen in fact *strengthened* so sharply against the dollar that it moved outside the *top* of the putative "target zone"—thus, more than 10 percent *above* its long-term norm—suggested for it by Williamson in his recent study on currency misalignments and the monetary system.[72]

On the other hand, there are instances where Japan has clearly seemed to manipulate the yen in a downward direction. In 1976, for example, the Japanese authorities bought huge amounts of dollars to keep the yen from

---

72. John Williamson, *The Exchange Rate System*, POLICY ANALYSES IN INTERNATIONAL ECONOMICS 5, 2d ed., rev. (Washington: Institute for International Economics, June 1985), p. 107; figure A8.

rising in the exchange market despite the emergence of a substantial surplus in their external accounts. Arguing that the surplus was a temporary result of the cyclical situation, the Japanese prevented market forces from carrying the yen upward until the new Carter administration insisted in early 1977 that they desist. This manipulative effort was an important cause of the huge (for then) Japanese surpluses and American deficits in 1977–78—including a fivefold rise in the bilateral Japanese surplus with the United States—which were in turn a major factor in the "dollar crisis" of 1978–79.[73]

Likewise, when the yen appreciated to record highs in the wake of the "free fall" of the dollar in 1978, Japan took several steps to promote capital outflow and (especially) limit capital inflow. Purchases of yen-denominated bonds by foreigners were banned, and reserve ratios on free yen deposits by nonresidents were introduced and raised during the year. These regulations were quickly lifted, however, after the US actions of November 1978 stabilized (and subsequently strengthened) the dollar.[74]

As a longer run matter, Japan has also tended until quite recently to resist international use of the yen. This has tended to discourage capital inflows to Japan, and may have depressed the exchange rate of the yen at least during some periods. The major "policy tool" to this end has been the lag in development of the Tokyo money market, whose shortage of liquid instruments (such as Treasury bills, bankers acceptances, and certificates of deposit) has limited the appeal of foreign investment in yen. It should be noted, however, that Germany and Switzerland, the other "new" reserve currency countries, exhibited similar reluctance to internationalize their currencies until the very late 1970s.

We are primarily concerned with the past four or five years, however, and during this period it is hard to find evidence of Japanese efforts to depress the yen. The major exceptions, paradoxically, relate to steps urged (forced?) on Japan by foreigners, notably the United States.

---

73. For a contemporary account that accurately predicted such results, see Bergsten's testimony before the House Banking Committee on 3 June 1976 and the Joint Economic Committee on 18 October 1976 and "Let's Avoid a Trade War," *Foreign Policy* (Summer 1976), all reprinted in C. Fred Bergsten, *Managing International Economic Interdependence: Selected Papers of C. Fred Bergsten: 1975–1976* (Lexington, Mass.: D.C. Heath and Co., 1977). Note, however, that such efforts are denied in Ryutaro Komiya and Miyako Suda, *Contemporary International Finance: Theory, History and Policy* (Tokyo: Nihon Keizai Shinbunsha, 1983).
74. Yoshitomi, *Japan as Capital Exporter*, p. 17.

First, the yen has *not* been a weak currency over the past few years. Largely as a result of the second oil shock, which produced large deficits in the Japanese current account in 1979–80, the real (i.e., inflation-adjusted) effective (i.e., trade-weighted) exchange rate of the yen weakened by about 30 percent from its high against the dollar in late 1978 to its low in early 1980. Since that time, however, the trade-weighted yen has risen by over 10 percent (even before the further run-up against the dollar *and* all other currencies after the Group of Five initiative on September 22, 1985).[75]

In essence, the yen has moved in a middle tier between the strong dollar and the weak continental European currencies. It remains undervalued against the dollar, though perhaps by no more than 10 percent at this writing (late September 1985). On the other hand, it has been at record highs against the DM and other continental European currencies for the past year or so. On balance, the yen has probably been undervalued by 10 percent to 15 percent through most of this period—and some observers would put the number substantially higher. But it seems no more (and perhaps a bit less) undervalued than the key European monies, implying again (as suggested in chapter 1) that the problem is primarily a generalized overvaluation of the dollar and casting strong doubt on the notion that Japan has been manipulating the yen downward.

Second, *direct* Japanese intervention in the exchange markets in recent years has been directed toward *resisting further weakening* of the yen. On numerous occasions, particularly when the dollar has been rising sharply, the Bank of Japan has bought yen to temper its decline. Indeed, the Bank of Japan would almost certainly have intervened more aggressively in this respect had American authorities been willing to participate in the effort in more than a token way—given the fact that the success of currency intervention relates importantly to the degree of cooperation (i.e., joint action) among the major central banks, particularly of the country whose currency (the dollar) is the primary focus of activity.[76]

Japan has implemented the September 22 agreement of the Group of Five far more aggressively than the other participants, at least in its early stages. During the first week of the effort the Bank of Japan reportedly sold well

---

75. Williamson, *The Exchange Rate System*, pp. 98–99.

76. Bonnie E. Loopesko, "Relationships Among Exchange Rates, Intervention and Interest Rates: An Empirical Investigation," *Journal of International Money and Finance* (December 1984), pp. 267–70.

over $1 billion and successfully drove the yen up by about 10 percent against the dollar. The most recent Japanese "manipulation" of the exchange rate clearly has been in a stabilizing direction.

Third, Japan in recent years appears to have kept its interest rates *higher* than called for by domestic considerations in order to *avoid* further weakening of the yen. It is frequently argued that Japanese interest rates are artificially low, thus promoting capital outflows and yen weakness, because of the extensive ceilings maintained on interest rates (including the widespread postal savings system) à la Regulation Q which had the same effect until eliminated in the United States. This view is buttressed by the observation that yen interest rates have been substantially lower than dollar interest rates in recent years—clearly an important factor in generating the huge flows of capital from Japan to the United States, which are the proximate cause of yen weakness against the dollar.[77]

Viewed within the Japanese domestic context, however, yen interest rates in recent years could not be regarded as low. Inflation in Japan, as measured by wholesale prices, has been virtually nonexistent since 1980. Even consumer prices have been rising annually at only 2 percent to 3 percent since 1981. Hence nominal short-term interest rates of 6 percent to 7 percent, the range maintained through most of this period, represent real rates of at least 3 percent to 4 percent—hardly a "low" level by any historical, or even contemporary, standards. (Long-term real rates have also recently been about 3 percent to 4 percent, closer to traditional levels but not below them.) Some Japanese and American economists (such as Masaru Yoshitomi and Lawrence Krause) have estimated that, seen in purely domestic terms, Japanese interest rates should have *declined* by 2 to 3 percentage points over the past couple of years.

Another indication of the *excessive* level of Japanese interest rates, in domestic Japanese terms, has been the steady (and increasingly insistent) call for *lower* rates by the business community and others concerned with speeding

---

77. These low interest rates were the major source of the interest expressed by numerous American businessmen in 1982–83 in "liberalization of the Japanese capital markets," which the Treasury Department pushed extremely hard in 1983–84. Unfortunately, as described in chapter 1, the predictable result was an increase in net capital outflow from Japan and a weaker yen—with adverse effects, at least in the short and medium run, on the prospects for most of the American businessmen who had proposed such "reforms." See Jeffrey A. Frankel, *The Yen/Dollar Agreement: Liberalizing Japanese Capital Markets*, POLICY ANALYSES IN INTERNATIONAL ECONOMICS 9 (Washington: Institute for International Economics, December 1984).

the pace of economic growth. The Bank of Japan has indeed found it necessary to respond publicly to these pressures on numerous occasions in resisting cuts in its discount rate—the benchmark for all Japanese interest rates. In doing so, it has cited primarily the need to avoid renewed depreciation of the yen in light of the increase in protectionist pressures against Japan which such depreciation would be likely to trigger.

There thus seem to have been offsetting forces at work on Japanese interest rates in recent years: structural factors tending to depress interest rates below market levels but policy decisions to keep them up. For the longer run, the ongoing deregulation of the Japanese financial system seems likely to eliminate the artifical depressants, just as Regulation Q and like ceilings have been abolished in this country. Hence "interest rate protection" of Japanese trade, like direct intervention in the exchange markets, seems not to have been a factor depressing the yen in the current situation nor likely to be one in the future.

As to internationalization of the yen, Japan has begun moving rapidly in the past few years. Prodded both by domestic financial evolution and the US Treasury, the Japanese money market is evolving toward world-class standards. A wide range of new money-market instruments—such as bankers acceptances and certificates of deposit, though not yet Treasury bills or commercial paper—have been instituted or will be within the next few years. The Japanese authorities are permitting Euro-yen transactions to increase rapidly. Any depressing effect on the yen exchange rate of the lack of an international role for the yen seems to be in the process of disappearing.[78]

There are three areas, however, where Japanese government actions have contributed in the recent past to the weakness of the yen against the dollar: the reduction of the budget deficit, the liberalization of capital outflows, and the restraints on the exports of certain products. As analyzed in chapter 2,

---

78. It should be noted that doubts exist as to the likely impact, over time, of yen internationalization on the exchange rate. C. Fred Bergsten and John Williamson, *The Multiple Reserve Currency System* (Washington: Institute for International Economics, forthcoming) have found that international use of an increasing number of national currencies has tended to affect the *volatility* of exchange rates much more than their average level. For example, the extreme weakness of the DM in recent years appears related to sales of DM from the stocks built up during its rapid internationalization in the late 1970s. The most that can be said is that the yen would probably strengthen in the early days of its greater global usage, as large stocks were built up abroad for the first time, but might fall below its equilibrium path at later stages when temporary weakness led to sell-offs from those stocks.

the fiscal tightening has helped to create a surplus of Japanese savings over domestic resource use and thus a net capital outflow that has weakened the yen and promoted Japan's large current account surplus. This action has clearly been taken for domestic reasons, however, and cannot be regarded as "manipulating" the yen. Ironically, the other two sets of measures have been largely pushed on Japan by other countries—notably the United States and the European Community—which have thus compounded their own trade and competitive problems.

Throughout most of the postwar period, Japan exercised tight controls on international movements of capital—particularly on outflows, to safeguard its exchange rate (mainly against excessive *weakening*) and its allegedly fragile currency reserves. During this period, however, Japanese wealth and incomes were rising at extremely rapid rates. Moreover, as discussed in chapter 2, Japanese savings rates are very high by international standards. Given standard portfolio diversification goals, there developed an enormous pent-up demand for foreign assets by Japanese investors. Liberalization of capital markets could thus have been expected to trigger sizable outflows until the standard stock adjustment could be completed. The relatively underdeveloped state of the Japanese capital markets, noted above and caused in part by the same history of controls, deterred an offsetting readjustment of foreign portfolios into yen assets.

Just such an effect, compounded substantially by the interest-rate differential in favor of the dollar throughout the 1980s, has occurred with the major Japanese liberalizations of 1980 and 1984. Gross Japanese capital exports have been averaging $5 billion to $6 billion *per month* in the recent past, and reached $8 billion monthly in the summer of 1985. Japanese insurance companies and pension trusts, in particular, are diversifying their portfolios substantially into foreign currency assets (over 70 percent of which are in dollars). And there may yet be more to come: the huge Japanese postal savings system, with the equivalent of over $300 billion in yen assets and annual increments to that total of at least 5 percent, wants to begin diversifying internationally as well but has not yet been permitted to do so to any significant extent. These capital flows are of course the proximate source of yen weakness against the dollar. The liberalization that promoted them is undoubtedly desirable from the long-term standpoint of both Japan and the world economy, but their timing could not have been worse because of their adverse impact on an already misaligned yen-dollar relationship.

The double irony in these events, from the standpoint of the US-Japan trade problem, is that the latest episode of capital liberalization has been (1) pushed on Japan largely by the US government (2) acting at least partly in response to pressure from American industrialists who believed that such liberalization would *help* American competitiveness. It would thus be difficult to charge Japan with using such steps to manipulate the yen downward.[79]

Japan's "voluntary" export restraints on a wide variety of products may also have served to hold the yen at a weaker level than called for by its underlying competitiveness. As with the liberalization of capital flows, quantification of the impact of this deliberalization is impossible. It has been estimated, however, that even an effective cut of $10 billion in Japanese exports by these restraints—a very conservative estimate of their real impact—could be holding the yen down by about 10 percentage points both in trade-weighted terms and against the dollar.[80] Paradoxically, then, American (and other foreign) exporters should seek the repeal of these restraints as promptly as possible to promote a stronger yen which would enhance their own competitive prospects in Japanese and third-country markets.

As with the liberalization of capital markets, one would have to take a very extreme view of Japan as both Machiavellian and unitary in its decision-making ("Japan, Inc.") to believe that these export restraints were adopted to promote yen weakness. The more straightforward interpretation, in both cases, is that the US government—operating at the time without any significant concern about strengthening the yen-dollar rate, and frequently in response to specific industry pressures (for example, money-center banks in the case of capital market liberalization, steel in the case of export restraints) rather than any overview of the national interest—has, once again, simply shot

---

79. The first major liberalization, announced in December 1980, was undertaken without any significant foreign pressure—although there was certainly no opposition from the United States or other countries, which mainly viewed the step as a belated Japanese effort to conform to the OECD Code of Capital Liberalization and, in general, free up capital markets like most of the other major industrial countries. One could conceivably charge Japan with liberalizing at that time to limit the substantial rise in the yen which had begun early in the year. However, there were no such intimations at the time and some Japanese themselves had major qualms about the step, coming so soon after the second oil shock had pushed their current account into deep deficit and led to the use of administrative guidance to sharply *reduce* capital outflows and *limit* the weakening of the yen at that time.

80. Williamson, *The Exchange Rate System*, pp. 80–82. On the other hand, as noted later in this chapter, an elimination of all existing trade barriers in the *two* countries would seem unlikely to change the level of their bilateral trade balance—and thus presumably the yen-dollar exchange rate—by very much.

itself in the foot. This conclusion is strengthened, of course, when one notes that the Treasury Department sent missions to Japan in 1984 to *promote* Japanese investments in US securities and has "tailored" its own securities to foreign tastes, thus weakening the yen further, and that US trade negotiators have recently pushed for *tighter* export restraints on Japan in some sectors (notably steel and textiles and apparel, though with some relaxation on autos as well).

In sum, there is no evidence that Japan is now practicing "exchange rate protection," although it apparently did so in the 1970s. Indeed, it has taken explicit steps—*buying* yen in the exchange markets, holding interest rates *above* levels called for by domestic circumstances, relaxing its previous resistance to internationalization of its currency—to avoid further weakening of the yen. To be sure, some Japanese policy actions—budget tightening, liberalization of capital outflows, and "voluntary" export restraints—have contributed to yen weakness, but these steps have been carried out for wholly domestic reasons or urged on Japan by other countries, notably the United States. Monetary protection cannot account for the imbalance in the US-Japan economic relationship.

Negotiating Objectives and Reciprocity

Absence of empirical evidence that Japan is highly protective does not of course mean that there are no protective barriers to reduce in Japan. The tangible cases of protection listed above (tables 3.1 and 3.2) are a point of departure, and in some sectors concrete discussions (Market-Oriented Sector-Specific or MOSS negotiations) are taking place on liberalizing less tangible dimensions of protection as well.

The political context of US negotiations with Japan is one of growing demands for "reciprocity," the idea that Japan should grant US businessmen access to Japanese markets in specific sectors, or even specific products, that is comparable to Japanese access to US markets in those same sectors or products. This section examines the list of product sectors in which US officials seek Japanese liberalization, and considers the current bilateral trade relationship in terms of reciprocity.

Because of the political importance of bilateral symmetry in trading opportunities, it is informative to return to the issue of bilateral trade balance in a broader context. Kenichi Ohmae of McKinsey Associates has compiled information on the activities of US affiliates in Japan and Japanese affiliates in the United States. These data indicate that, because US firms have been much more active to date in Japan than Japanese firms have been in the United States, the total size of market presence shows a much closer bilateral symmetry than do the trade flows alone.

Table 3.8 reports these estimates, along with appropriate data on bilateral trade. Total sales of US firms to Japan are estimated as the sum of US exports (f.o.b.) and the sales of US affiliates in Japan. Only that portion of total affiliate sales corresponding to the equity position of US firms in their affiliate is included. On this basis, total sales of US firms to the Japanese market amounted to $55 billion in 1984. Of this total, direct exports were 43 percent, with affiliate sales accounting for 57 percent.

By contrast, of total sales by Japanese firms to the US market ($71 billion), 86 percent were direct exports. Only 14 percent, or $10 billion, took the form of sales of Japanese affiliates (equity share basis) in the US market. Thus, consideration of trade data alone tends to exaggerate the asymmetry in market penetration between the United States and Japan. Incorporation of sales by affiliated firms reveals that, in absolute dollar terms, US penetration into the Japanese market is approximately four-fifths as large as Japanese penetration into the US market (instead of two-fifths as implied by trade data alone).[81] Correspondingly, the US bilateral deficit on total activity is only $15 billion, instead of the $37 billion on direct trade.

The bilateral balance on market presence (or penetration) has different economic implications from those of the trade balance. Direct exports generate domestic jobs and value added from capital, while activity by foreign affiliates generates only profits to the home firm and country (although it may stimulate home firm exports, already included in the trade balance). Nevertheless, much of the argument on the Japanese economy is couched in terms of its oligopolistic closedness to foreigners. In the dimension of strategic behavior of firms, it is fully relevant to incorporate the activity of foreign affiliates; to omit this activity seriously understates the performance of US firms.

---

81. Relative to GNP, US penetration of the Japanese market is actually higher than Japan's penetration of the US market. Thus, the figures in table 3.8 imply total US sales to Japan equivalent to 4.5 percent of Japan's GNP, and sales by Japanese firms equal to 2.1 percent of US GNP. IMF, *International Financial Statistics*, May 1985. However, this divergence primarily reflects the different sizes of the two economies, not discrepancies in market access. In balanced transactions between a larger and a smaller economy, the flows will always be a larger fraction of the GNP of the smaller country.

TABLE 3.8   **US-Japanese bilateral market penetration, including exports and sales of foreign affiliates, 1984 (billion dollars)**

	US sales to Japan	Japanese sales to United States	Balance
Exports, f.o.b.	23.58	60.43	−36.85
Sales of foreign affiliates			
Total	43.90	12.80	31.10
Equity portion[a]	31.70	10.20	21.50
Total, exports plus affiliate sales (equity basis)	55.28	70.63	−15.35

Source: US Department of Commerce, *Highlights of US Export and Import Trade,* December 1984; IMF; and Kenichi Ohmae, Managing Director, McKinsey, Tokyo: speech to National Press Club, Washington, 17 April 1985.
a. Equity position: US holdings in Japan, 72.2 percent; Japanese holdings in the United States, 80.0 percent.

It is the trade deficit itself that has dominated policy discussion and congressional attitudes, however. The bilateral deficit seems to many to be direct evidence that the United States does not have access to the Japanese market comparable to Japanese access to the US market. From this general plane the policy discussion in recent months has narrowed to certain key sectors in which Japan is perceived to be protective.

One sector is telecommunications, for which a common perception is that Japanese restrictions must account for the large US deficit in bilateral trade in light of the perceived technological superiority of US firms. Thus, in 1984, US telecommunications exports to Japan amounted to $224 million, compared with $3.3 billion in US imports from Japan.[82] In addition to telecommunications, US negotiators have recently focused their efforts on liberalization of Japan's market for electronics, pharmaceuticals and medical equipment, and wood and forest products.

In telecommunications, US negotiators have sought administrative procedures that would ensure that Japan's technical standards are not used as a

---

82. "Trade War Ahead?" *Newsweek,* 15 April 1985, p. 22.

barrier to imports.[83] With the recent privatization of the Nippon Telephone and Telegraph Company, the issue has also taken on aspects of private oligopoly practice.

In sophisticated electronics, US authorities have sought protection of copyright protection for US computer software, American participation in development of industrial standards, acceptance of US test data, access for American companies to research sponsored by the Japanese government, and revision of foreign exchange controls limiting Japanese purchases. In pharmaceuticals and medical equipment, the issue has been allowance of foreign test data. In forestry products, Japan has maintained relatively high tariffs, with the effect of curtailing US exports of plywood and paper.[84]

Although US negotiating efforts in recent months have focused on these specific areas, US officials have sought Japanese liberalization of a wider range of goods. In early 1985, administration officials stated that US exports to Japan would rise by $10 billion annually if Japan would eliminate its tariff and nontariff barriers.[85] Table 3.9 presents estimates by the Department of Commerce that appear to lie behind the figure of $10 billion.[86]

These estimates are based on the premise that, in the absence of Japanese protection, US exports would hold the same share of the Japanese market as the world market. However, in several cases, the Commerce estimates override this methodology with a higher figure based on estimates by the industry or by negotiators. The total estimate for the 20 product sectors[87] is that US exports of goods and services would rise by approximately $17 billion if Japanese protection were eliminated. This range is far higher than in many private estimates.[88] US officials have referred more cautiously to a

---

83. US negotiators sought to obtain direct representation by a US-affiliated company in Japan on the council that advises the government on telecommunications policy; they sought a reduction in the number of standards; and they urged elimination of the requirement that foreign equipment be approved and registered before it can be used. Prime Minister Nakasone agreed to all of their requests. *Washington Post,* 2 April 1985; and *Wall Street Journal,* 3 April 1985.

84. *Washington Post,* 10 April 1985; *Wall Street Journal,* 10 April 1985.

85. *Washington Post,* 8 February 1985.

86. Communication with staff of the Department of Commerce indicates that the estimates should be interpreted as rough approximations.

87. Note that the absence of automobiles from the Commerce list tends to confirm the judgment above that the sector should be omitted from an enumeration of sectors with major nontariff barriers (table 3.2).

88. For example, in an earlier survey of several independent studies, Saxonhouse concluded that the loss of US exports to Japan's protection amounted to $1 billion to $2 billion annually. Saxonhouse, "The Micro- and Macroeconomics of Foreign Sales to Japan," p. 264.

TABLE 3.9   **Potential increase in US exports from trade liberalization by Japan, alternative estimates (million dollars)**

Sector	US market share (percentage)		Japanese market[a]
	World	Japan	
Telecommunications	2.4	6.1	4,000
Paper	5.6	5.8	n.a.
Wood products	0.8	12.0	n.a.
Electronic components	20.0	7.0	8,300
Computers	32.0	13.0	5,500
Medical equipment	n.a.	7.0	2,700
Pharmaceuticals	4.8	3.0	17,000
Cigarettes	1.5[c]	0.7–1.8	12,300
Chemicals	4.6	2.0	55,000
Cosmetics	1.5	0.2	8,000
Confectionery (chocolate)[e]	n.a.	n.a.	10
Aluminum[e]	n.a.	1.0–16.0	n.a.
Machine tools	6.2	2.3	4,400
Fish[h]	n.a.	4.2	15,600
Beef[h]	n.a.	33.0	n.a.
Citrus	n.a.	n.a.	n.a.
Oil	1.1	0.9	46,542[i]
Gas	0.5	6.0	n.a.
Coal	27.0	21.0	n.a.
Insurance, brokerage, mutual funds	n.a.	n.a.	n.a.
Total			

Source: Unofficial Commerce Department estimates (4 April 1985), and authors' calculations (see text).

a. In most cases, 1982.
b. In absence of data, applies Commerce estimate.
c. All tobacco products.
d. Applies 1.5 *minus* 0.7 percent market share differential.
e. If tariffs are reduced to US level.
f. By 1990.
g. Arbitrarily 10 percent of market.
h. If quotas are eliminated.
i. Physical volume evaluated at $28 per barrel.

	Potential additional US exports	
Commerce	Alternative A	Alternative B
750	0	0
500	0	0
1,500	0	0
1,075	1,075	537
1,075	1,045	537
400	400[b]	200
350	306	153
1,900	98[d]	98[d]
1,500	1,430	725
1,500	104	52
67[f]	1[g]	1
100	100[b]	100
175	172	86
400	400[b]	400
280	280[b]	280
40	40[b]	40
2,000	93	93
2,000	0	0
1,000	1,000[b]	1,000
300	300[b]	150
16,912	6,844	4,452

figure of $10 billion, in part because $2 billion of the $17 billion total is attributable to a US restriction on oil exports from Alaska (as discussed above) instead of Japanese protection.

It is of interest to examine the estimates that would have been reached if the Commerce analysts had adhered strictly to the methodology of applying the global market share of US exports to the Japanese market. Table 3.9 presents this set of estimates as "Alternative A." Interestingly, the US market share in Japan already exceeds the global market share in telecommunications, paper, wood products, and gas, so that Alternative A yields zero estimates in these sectors. In seven other sectors no data on market shares are available, and Alternative A merely represents the Commerce estimates. The total increase of US exports under a strict application of the market-share methodology applied in principle by Commerce itself would amount to $6.8 billion, or $10 billion less than the department's estimate.

More fundamentally, the market-share methodology ignores the principle of comparative advantage. One would not expect the US share in Japan's market for manufactures to be as high as the share in the global market because of Japan's strong comparative advantage in manufactures, as discussed above. Accordingly, Alternative B in the table attempts to adjust for comparative advantage. In all manufactured goods and in services, Alternative B arbitrarily cuts the estimated increase in US exports under Alternative A by half. However, in all sectors based on natural resources, Alternative B accepts the estimate found in Alternative A. As indicated in the table, after this rough adjustment for comparative advantage, the total estimated increase in US exports would be $4.5 billion.

These estimates understate the impact of liberalization in agricultural products by excluding rice. The acute concern in Japan for self-sufficiency in rice has led to high protection in this sector, at domestic prices as much as 400 percent above international prices.[89] The experience of the US embargo on soybean exports in 1973 has probably added to Japan's reluctance to become highly dependent on imports for its principal dietary staple. A radical but not complete liberalization of rice imports might increase the import share to one-half of total consumption of approximately 13 million metric

---

89. Michael R. Reich, Yasuo Endo, and C. Peter Timmer, "The Political Economy of Structural Change: Conflict Between Japanese and United States Agricultural Policy" (Cambridge, Mass.: Harvard University, 25 June 1985; processed), p. 25.

tons annually. If the US share in the supply of imports were 30 percent, the resulting increase in US exports would be approximately $700 million annually.[90]

The complete omission of wood products, as in alternative estimates A and B, might also cause an understatement of the potential impact of liberalization. Tariffs in the range of 15 percent have been an obstacle to imports of plywood. However, for rough wood products, imports into Japan are generally duty free.[91] In 1982 Japan's imports of wood products from the United States amounted to $1.64 billion for wood chips and roughly squared wood, while imports of plywood were only $17.5 million.[92] Even if the tariff on plywood were cut to zero, and if Japan's imports from the United States rose by a large percentage, such as 50 percent, US export gains would be minimal (in this example, only about $9 million). In practice, then, wood products may be omitted from the calculations of protective effect, from the standpoint of tariff protection.

The estimates for cigarettes also warrant attention. Application of the market-shares approach implies a potential increase of approximately $100 million in US cigarette exports to Japan. In contrast, the Commerce estimates suggest that US exports could rise by $1.9 billion, from a 1982 base of $80 million. This 25-fold mushrooming of imports is premised on an increase of US exports to a share of 16 percent in the Japanese market. These large expectations may be behind the decision of the Reagan administration to

90. Hufbauer and Schott use a figure of $1 billion, assuming total imports would rise as high as 9 million metric tons annually. Based on interviews with trade associations and other observers of US-Japanese trade, they also conclude that total US exports to Japan could expand by $10.5 billion, from elimination of Japanese protection, somewhat higher than the results derived here. Gary Clyde Hufbauer and Jeffrey J. Schott, *Trading for Growth: The Next Round of Trade Negotiations,* POLICY ANALYSES IN INTERNATIONAL ECONOMICS 11 (Washington: Institute for International Economics, September 1985), p. 31. Note that government subsidies in wheat and barley also increase the share of domestic production in consumption of these grains (13 percent in 1982) above levels they would otherwise attain. However, cutting domestic production in half would increase US exports of wheat and barley by only about $80 million annually. Calculated from Shailendra J. Anjaria, Naheed Kirmani, and Arne B. Petersen, *Trade Policy Issues and Developments* (Washington: International Monetary Fund, 1985), p. 64; OECD, *Trade by Commodities,* series C, January–December 1980, pp. 182–85; and IMF, *International Financial Statistics,* September 1985, p. 76.
91. By communication, Japanese Embassy, Washington.
92. SITC groups 24 and 63, respectively. OECD, *Foreign Trade by Commodities,* series C, 1982, pp. 132, 183.

initiate an unfair trade investigation (under section 301 of the 1974 Trade Act) on Japanese imports of cigarettes (chapter 1). However, the basis for these expectations is questionable. Japan had already liberalized the cigarette market in April 1985 by ending the government monopoly and opening distribution to competition.[93] Although a 20 percent tariff remains on cigarettes, the import base is too small to make its removal capable of increasing imports by such a substantial sum.

With the addition of rice, Alternatives A and B (table 3.9) would reach $7.5 billion and $5.2 billion, respectively, as the range for increased US exports to Japan resulting from liberalization of the Japanese market. This range of roughly $5 billion to $8 billion is our central estimate for the impact of Japanese liberalization on US exports. It should be noted that, by the nature of the market-shares approach, this estimate implicitly calculates the effect of a reduction in Japanese protection to the average level for other countries—not a complete elimination of protection. However, this estimate does not make allowance for second-round effects, such as the reduction in tobacco imports as cigarette imports are liberalized, or the reduction in US exports following the likely depreciation of the yen that would be induced by a reduction in Japan's trade surplus (in the absence of any correction in the saving-investment imbalances in the two countries).

As noted above, it is important to distinguish between protection caused by government action and that resulting from general influences of economic structure. The latter may be beyond the government's control. The categories in table 3.9 that represent government obstacles to imports include: fish, rice, beef, and citrus (quotas); medical equipment, pharmaceuticals, cosmetics (Ministry of Health and Welfare licensing and standards, and patent obstacles); and services (Ministry of Finance regulation of insurance).[94] The categories with barriers strictly or primarily from economic structure rather than from the government include electronics components (keiretsu reciprocal purchasing), chemicals (keiretsu control of pipelines and unloading in petrochemicals), gas, coal, aluminum (now that a 17 percent tariff has been eliminated), and machine tools (keiretsu). Categories with a joint role of government and economic structure in protection include telecommunications (government

---

93. *Washington Post*, 9 September 1985.
94. The division between government and structural barriers is based primarily on the nature of the trade obstacle in each sector as described by Commerce Department experts, by communication.

nonprocurement of foreign satellites; psychological barriers to imports in the newly private NTT; lack of multinational presence and therefore infrastructure, partly because of difficulty of takeover under Japanese corporate law); paper (depressed industry with strong industry association and MITI guidance); wood (tariffs on plywood; industry obstacles such as standard sizes of wood products, and distribution obstacles); tobacco (20 percent tariff; remainder structural); and processed foods (health standards; small-outlet distribution system).

Overall, and using the Commerce Department basis in table 3.9, the potential impact of Japan's liberalization on US exports breaks down as follows: measures under direct government control, $4.6 billion; protection resulting from economic structure, $10.3 billion.[95] If instead Alternative B (table 3.9) is used as the basis, the division is as follows: governmental, $1.5 billion; structural, $3 billion. Adding rice brings the total under governmental control to $2.2 billion.

These estimates suggest that only about one-third of potential liberalization is directly under the government's control—a potential increase in US exports ranging only from approximately $2.2 billion (Alternative B basis plus rice) to $5 billion (Commerce basis). This modest range implies that there is a risk that even with the most determined liberalization by the Japanese government, the impact on the trade balance could be too small to avoid continued frustration on the part of US legislators and businessmen.

Finally, the magnitude of the trade impact of Japan's protection may be put into perspective by considering the size of the trade base. In 1984 US exports to Japan were $23.6 billion (table 2.7, chapter 2). If the full Commerce Department estimate of $17 billion is accepted as the impact of Japan's protection, liberalization would bring a remarkable 72 percent increase in US exports to Japan. Even assuming a relatively high import price elasticity of 1.5 (the estimate in appendix B suggests the elasticity is 1.2), this diagnosis would imply that the tariff-equivalent of Japan's protection is 92 percent.[96] It is difficult to believe that Japan's protection is anywhere near this high.

---

95. The figures omit the $2 billion associated with US controls on Alaskan oil exports. The division between governmental and structural barriers for those products in which both are present is based on judgmental allocation, including rough estimates of tariff effects where the tariff is the principal governmental obstacle. Adding rice brings the governmentally controlled estimate to $5.3 billion (Commerce basis) or $2.2 billion (Alternative B basis).

96. Elimination of the protection would reduce import prices by $t/(1 + t)$, where t is the tariff equivalent. Thus, $(1.5) [t/(1 + t)] = 0.72$, and $t = 0.92$.

Even the central estimates suggested here for the protective effect of Japan's protection, $5 billion to $8 billion, would imply that liberalization would increase US exports by about 30 percent. This substantial increase would in turn imply relatively high protection: a tariff-equivalent of 25 percent.[97] However, as a working hypothesis, a level of overall Japanese protection equivalent to a tariff of nearly 25 percent is far more credible then a tariff-equivalent of over 90 percent.

US Protection

In view of the strong emphasis on market reciprocity, it is informative to consider as well the increase in US imports from Japan that could be expected from liberalization of the US market. At the outset, it should be noted that US protection is generally more transparent than protection in Japan. As noted above, the United States relies on tariffs and quotas rather than licensing, standards, and other devices more subject to bureaucratic manipulation. Moreover, few charges are leveled against societal or cultural features of American life as working to restrict purchases from abroad.[98] Hence, we do not search for tacit protection in the United States as we do for Japan, confining this analysis to the apparent controls in several major industries.

Automobiles and steel are the two key sectors of US protection against Japan. In automobiles, the Japanese government has increased the voluntary quota by 24 percent—from 1.9 million units to 2.3 million, for an increase of 450,000 units.[99] In early 1985, US Trade Representative William E. Brock stated that complete elimination of the voluntary export quotas would raise US imports from Japan by 750,000 units annually.[100] Accordingly, the voluntary quotas that still remained after Japan's liberalization in April 1985

---

97. $(1.5) [t/(1 + t)] = 0.30; t = 0.25$.
98. However, there are also anecdotes about such behavior in the United States. For example, the chairman of one of America's leading automobile companies reportedly rejected the advice of his top staff to save considerable amounts of money in the 1970s by purchasing steel from Japan on the grounds that "we buy all our steel from American companies." More recently, a major US grain-trading firm reportedly backed off from a plan to import wheat from Argentina (an anomalous opportunity provided by the overvalued dollar and sharp Argentine devaluations) as the result of pressure from a US agency.
99. *Wall Street Journal,* 26 April 1985.
100. *Wall Street Journal,* 21 February 1985.

would appear to have a protective effect, reducing Japan's exports by 300,000 automobiles per year. With an average import value of $6,337 per vehicle,[101] complete liberalization would increase US imports of automobiles from Japan by $1.9 billion.

In steel, Japan appears to have maintained a tacit voluntary export quota limiting exports to the United States to 6 million tons since at least 1978.[102] In addition, the new overt regime of "voluntary" export quotas negotiated with major suppliers since late 1984 has further limited imports from Japan.

Japanese efficiency in steel production is well known. Its integrated steel mills are large-scale, modern, energy-efficient, and typically located by deepwater ports. By contrast, many US plants are older and operate at smaller, less efficient scale; in addition, US wages have risen substantially relative to the US manufacturing average. Alternative estimates place the resulting excess cost of US producers above Japanese production in a range of 20 percent to 30 percent, even in a year such as 1980 when the dollar was not overvalued.[103]

A central estimate for the price elasticity (responsiveness) of US steel imports would appear to be approximately −2.5.[104] Complete liberalization of US steel imports from Japan, including not only elimination of the new quota but also a change in the protective environment such that Japanese producers no longer felt compelled to limit exports to the 6-million-ton range of the last several years, would increase US imports substantially. The bilateral quota arranged in 1984 cut Japan's market share from 6.8 percent of US apparent consumption in 1984 to 5.8 percent. Thus, merely reversing the new quota decision would increase the volume of imports by 17 percent from their expected 1985 base of 5.6 million tons.[105] In addition, assuming that prices of Japanese steel to US importers would fall by 15 percent in a

101. US International Trade Commission, *The Automobile Industry: Monthly Report on Selected Economic Indicators,* USITC Publication No. 1650 (Washington, February 1985), p. 2.

102. Ingo Walter, "Structural Adjustment and Trade Policy in the International Steel Industry," in *Trade Policy in the 1980s,* edited by William R. Cline, p. 495.

103. Congressional Budget Office (CBO), *The Effects of Import Quotas on the Steel Industry* (Washington, July 1984), p. 28.

104. William R. Cline, "U.S. Trade and Industrial Policy: The Experience of Textiles, Steel, and Automobiles" (paper presented at the Export–Import Bank 50th Anniversary Conference, "Trade '84," 25–26 October 1984, Washington; processed).

105. US International Trade Commission, *Monthly Report on Selected Steel Industry Data,* USITC Publication No. 1700 (Washington, May 1985), and USITC staff communication.

liberalized environment (still leaving perhaps a 10 percent to 15 percent differential in view of such factors as greater facility of supply from nearby domestic producers), the volume of Japan's steel exports to the United States would rise by 37 percent (applying the demand elacticity of -2.5). The combined effect would be an increase of 60 percent in Japan's steel exports, or from 5.7 million tons (1984) to 9.1 million tons. At an average price of approximately $500 per ton,[106] the increase of 3.4 million tons would mean a rise in US steel imports from Japan by $1.7 billion annually.

Finally, Japan is the only industrial country against which the United States maintains textile and apparel quotas under the Multi-Fiber Arrangement.[107] Recent estimates by Tarr and Morkre indicate that the elimination of quotas on textile-apparel imports from Hong Kong would increase the volume of these imports by between 28 percent and 85 percent.[108] Applying an average of 56 percent to the 1984 base value of US imports from Japan ($1.24 billion),[109] elimination of US textile quotas against Japan would increase Japanese exports by an estimated $690 million.[110]

In sum, liberalization of current protection in the US market for automobiles, steel, and textiles would increase Japan's exports by $1.9 billion, $1.7 billion, and $690 million, respectively, for a total of $4.3 billion. This estimate is between one-half and four-fifths of the total ($5 billion to $8 billion) estimated for the impact on US exports from thorough liberalization of Japan's imports, and it equals or exceeds the magnitude estimated for

---

106. CBO, *The Effects of Import Quotas*, p. 42.

107. Eighteen import categories representing 360 million square yards are under quotas, with the remaining categories subject to consultation. US International Trade Commission, *US Imports of Textile and Apparel Products under the Multifiber Arrangement, January–June 1984*, USITC Publication No. 1635 (Washington, January 1985), pp. A–1 to A–3.

108. Calculated from tables 5.1 and 5.3 of David G. Tarr and Morris E. Morkre, *Aggregate Costs to the United States of Tariffs and Quotas on Imports: General Tariff Cuts and Removal of Quotas on Automobiles, Steel, Sugar, and Textiles* (Washington: Federal Trade Commission, December 1984).

109. US Department of Commerce, *Highlights of US Export and Import Trade*, FT 990, December 1984, p. C–13.

110. This estimate may be overstated because Japan may not be as competitive in textiles and apparel as Hong Kong. However, the broader point is that US textile-apparel protection against all sources is high while Japan does not maintain overt barriers and is itself a controlled country under the MFA, so that liberalization of textiles and apparel across the board would increase US imports far more than Japan's.

protection directly within the Japanese government's control ($2.5 billion to $5 billion).

Because of the inevitable roughness of the estimates, we would stop short of asserting that "protection parity" exists between Japan and the United States. In addition, US protection is clearly more transparent than that of Japan. Moreover, as noted above, the widespread perception of Japanese protection may also affect trade flows subtly by deterring export efforts by American (and other foreign) firms. And the base of US imports from Japan is almost three times as large as the base of Japan's imports from the United States—so that even identical magnitudes of trade change from liberalization of existing barriers, in dollar terms, would imply a much higher tariff equivalent in Japan than in the United States (because of the larger percentage change in imports from liberalization).

We would conclude, however, that the difference in protection between the two countries is not nearly great enough to justify the shrill calls for "reciprocity" which imply that the playing field is tilted sharply against the United States. It is clear that any difference that does exist can explain, at most, a modest part of the bilateral trade imbalance or even its growth in recent years. We strongly advocate efforts to reduce existing barriers, in both countries, and to avoid erecting new ones (especially in the name of achieving "reciprocity" through unilateral actions). But trade liberalization should be done in the context of a comprehensive attack on the real sources of the US trade deficit, as well, to which we now turn in our concluding chapter.

4 Conclusion and Policy Recommendations

This chapter presents a package of policy recommendations to deal with the US-Japan economic problem, several of which are updated to the end of 1986 in the postscript. The measures suggested include both macroeconomic and microeconomic actions. Before turning to these specific proposals, however, it may be useful to recapitulate the analytical findings of chapters 2 and 3 on which they are based.

Analytical Summary

Despite the focus of political attention on Japan's import protection, the evidence is overwhelming that the large rise in the US-Japan bilateral trade deficit in recent years (from $12 billion in 1980 to $37 billion in 1984 and as much as $50 billion in 1985) has been caused by macroeconomic factors:

• Since 1980, 17 of 25 major US trading partners have had even larger increases in their bilateral trade balances with the United States than Japan, relative to the base of bilateral trade with each. This pattern indicates the problem is not specific to Japan but is instead a more widespread reflection of US economic distortions.

• The overall US external imbalance (current account deficit of nearly $100 billion in 1984, probably $125 billion in 1985) is driven by its domestic imbalance between resources available from savings and resources used for private investment and government deficits. Resources from abroad (net imports of goods and services and capital inflows) are required to fill this gap. The US fiscal balance shifted from a surplus of 0.6 percent of GNP in 1979 to a deficit of 3.8 percent in 1982–84, while domestic savings and investment remained relatively constant (despite a temporary but severe dip in investment in the 1982 recession). A fiscal bust (rather than an investment boom) spurred the widening resource gap, to almost 3 percent of GNP, creating an external deficit of like magnitude.

121

• Japan's overall external surplus (perhaps $50 billion in 1985) derives from a domestic imbalance in the opposite direction. Japan's high domestic savings and declining investment have meant a resource surplus that has created a huge external surplus. While high fiscal deficits in the late 1970s absorbed much of this excess saving, by 1984 the move toward fiscal restraint in Japan had left a net domestic resource surplus of also about 3 percent of GNP.

• Without action on the fundamentals to reduce these imbalances, it will be difficult to resolve the US-Japan problem (except at great economic cost through increased interest rates and lower investment in the United States). Cuts in US fiscal deficits are essential. With a corrected US resource balance, there would be some natural tendency for Japan's resource surplus to diminish, and its trade surplus with the United States would decline, but action to spur investment (or reduce savings) in Japan will be necessary as well.

• Realistic targets for the US-Japan trade balance should recognize that, because of the triangular nature of this trade, an ongoing bilateral deficit will exist even when both countries are in overall equilibrium. With limited natural resources, Japan relies heavily on imports of oil and other raw materials (with a heavier emphasis on supply from members of the Organization of Petroleum Exporting Countries, OPEC, and from developing countries) and exports of manufactures to pay for them (with a heavier emphasis on US markets). From 1977 to 1983, the US share in Japan's exports was 26.1 percent and its share in Japan's imports was 18.3 percent. If Japan runs a current account (and trade) surplus of 1 percent to 1.5 percent of GNP, as may be expected from the structure of its underlying saving-investment relationship, application of these (triangular) trade shares means that the structural bilateral deficit in US-Japanese trade will be $20 billion to $25 billion annually (taking account of higher dollar prices of Japan's exports after dollar correction).

• The proximate instrument driving the trade balance is the exchange rate. The US fiscal deficit and resource gap have driven up interest rates, inducing capital inflow (and reducing capital outflow). Higher net inflows of capital have bid up the price of the dollar relative to other currencies. In 1984 the dollar was overvalued relative to the yen by over 20 percent, relative to underlying competitive conditions between the two countries.

• The strong dollar has increased US imports from Japan and decreased US exports. A 10 percent real depreciation of the dollar against the yen would cut the current dollar value of imports by just under 10 percent, and would increase US exports to Japan by about 12 percent (appendix B). Each 10 percent depreciation of the dollar thus reduces US imports by about $5.6 billion and increases US exports by about $2.7 billion, for a total improvement of over $8 billion in the bilateral trade balance.

• A statistically estimated model shows that, if the dollar and yen had been at equilibrium rates in 1980–84, the bilateral deficit by 1984 would have been $23 billion instead of $37 billion. At equilibrium exchange rates, US imports from Japan would have risen by about 50 percent instead of more than 80 percent from 1980 to 1984 in current dollars (and by 35 percent instead of more than 90 percent in physical volume). US exports would have risen by over 50 percent in value, instead of only 12 percent. If, in addition, Japan's growth had been slightly higher to match its earlier excess above US rates (1.8 percent gap), the 1984 bilateral deficit would have been cut further by about $1½ billion.

• These calculations indicate that virtually the entire increase in the bilateral deficit in recent years can be explained by macroeconomic influences, primarily the overvaluation of the dollar. Increased Japanese protection has not played a role in the widening of the deficit. Nonetheless, the existing *level* of Japanese protection is widely believed to be extremely high and some advocate retaliatory protection if Japan does not reduce its barriers.

Analytical evaluation of Japan's protection (chapter 3) does not confirm the common view that protection is far greater in Japan than in the United States and other industrial countries:

• Data on *overt* tariff and nontariff barriers indicate that direct protection in Japan is no higher, and may be lower, than that in the United States. Even when agriculture (more heavily protected in Japan) is included, Japan's overt nontariff barriers do not cover a wider share of trade than those in the United States (which protects manufactures more heavily by such barriers). However, the data available do not indicate the severity (as opposed to product coverage) of nontariff trade barriers. Moreover, American protection tends to be much more transparent than that in Japan.

• Many informed critics of Japan recognize that its overt barriers may be no more extensive than those in the United States but hold that Japan's main protection is in indirect forms, including industrial targeting, regulation, product standards, government procurement, and oligopoly behavior by *keiretsu* conglomerates. Review of anecdotal information indicates strong suspicion of Japanese indirect protection. This perception may itself be a barrier to willingness of US firms to attempt to export. In addition, Japan's emphasis on infant-industry intervention, as highlighted by case-history studies, raises problems for trading partners.

• Indirect evidence on the scope of such protection may be revealed by the ratio of imports to GNP: if protection is unusually severe, this ratio should be abnormally low. However, data for the industrial countries (1974–84) show that Japan's ratio of imports to GNP is almost precisely what would be expected for a country of its economic size (figure 3.1). Statistical tests incorporating transport costs and natural resource endowments confirm that Japan's import-GNP ratio is normal by international standards.

• A low share of manufactured goods in Japan's total imports appears to reflect its comparative disadvantage in natural resources rather than protection. Intra-industry trade is largely consistent with international patterns. US manufactured exports to Japan exceed those to Germany (often cited as a free-trade country) in absolute and relative terms. Japan's imports of manufactures from developing countries are not unusually low if a wide definition of such products (including processed foods and copper) is used.

• Japan has not used the exchange rate as a protective device, and has recently tried to strengthen, rather than weaken, the yen.

• In early 1985, US officials publicly estimated the extent of Japan's protective effect on US exports at $10 billion. Unofficial working estimates from the Commerce Department enumerated product categories totaling $17 billion in protective effect. Adjustments of these estimates to reflect a more consistent methodology, and to allow for Japanese comparative advantage in manufactures, place our central estimate of the protective effect of Japan's barriers at $5 billion to $8 billion in adverse impact on US exports annually. Of this amount, perhaps one-third is from barriers directly under the control of the Japanese government. The rest derives from structural features of the economy such as the keiretsu.

• Obstacles to US imports from Japan in steel, textiles, and automobiles reduce our imports by approximately $4 billion annually. The embargo on exports of Alaskan oil may limit exports by $2 billion or more.

• The impact of Japan's barriers on US exports is limited relative to the total bilateral deficit of nearly $50 billion, especially if the corresponding effect of US barriers on the bilateral balance is taken into account. It would be highly desirable to reduce, and eventually eliminate, these obstacles to trade in both countries. However, trade retaliation on grounds of reciprocity would not go far to correct the imbalance, and would not appear to be warranted in terms of the aggregate impact of each country's existing restraints.

The Policy Setting

As noted, the analysis in chapter 2 suggests that Japan will tend to run a sizable bilateral current account surplus with the United States, for at least the next few years on the order of perhaps $20 billion to $25 billion, even when both countries are in global equilibrium.[1] Recently, however, both the global and bilateral imbalances of the two countries have soared to much higher levels: $50 billion for the Japanese global surplus and the bilateral imbalance; perhaps $125 billion in 1985 for the American global deficit. The sharp escalation of the US-Japan economic problem derives from the magnitude of, and huge increase in, the global current account imbalances of the two countries and the resulting bilateral imbalance between them.

Virtually all of the sharp *rise* in these global imbalances since 1980 can in turn be explained by exchange rate changes (and, in 1983 and early 1984, by faster economic growth in the United States). In particular, from two-thirds to three-fourths of the increase in the overall American current account deficit can be traced to the rise of the dollar.[2] The primary cause of the present crisis thus seems to lie with the macroeconomic policies of the two

---

1. As indicated in chapter 2, "global equilibrium" for Japan probably means a surplus on the current account of perhaps 1½ percent of GNP, or about $20 to $25 billion annually, allowing for some increase in dollar prices after correction of the dollar, approximately the same as its bilateral surplus with the United States for at least the next few years. The meaning of "global equilibrium" for the United States is much more difficult to determine; some analysts believe that a surplus will be needed, to regain market confidence after the huge deficits of the current period and to service the substantial net debtor position that is emerging, while others believe that a moderate deficit (by current standards) can be sustained indefinitely because of ongoing foreign desires to place new investments in dollar assets, albeit at a slower pace than of late.

2. Stephen Marris, *Deficits and the Dollar: The World Economy at Risk* POLICY ANALYSES IN INTERNATIONAL ECONOMICS 14 (Washington: Institute for International Economics, December 1985), chapter 3.

countries, perhaps along with their underlying economic structures. Trade *policy,* as usually defined, cannot have much impact on the trade *imbalances.*[3]

Moreover, the level of the two countries' international imbalances both globally and with each other may rise further in the coming year or so. Even the most effective *policy* responses to the macroeconomic and sector-specific aspects of the problem will take some time to produce significant changes in trade *flows.* For example, even a complete correction of the yen/dollar misalignment by the end of 1985 would not be significantly reflected in the trade data until late 1986 or 1987. By definition, structural change in either country will take considerable time. It is thus essential to address all components of the issue with great urgency, especially its macroeconomics, to begin the process of correction and attempt to head off destructive policy responses.

Fortunately, policy changes—particularly with respect to budgets in the two countries—are available which offer promise of achieving such results. Curiously, however, it is at the level of macroeconomic policy where there has apparently been the least dialogue between the two countries. To be sure, each US-Japan communiqué has included ritual references to the need to reduce US budget deficits. But, apart from limited discussion around the time of the Reagan-Nakasone summit in November 1983 and the run-up to the Bonn summit of 1985, there seems to have been no serious US effort to prod Japanese macroeconomic policy in the needed direction. Partly as a result, the prospects for altering macroeconomic policies are not very promising, and we therefore emphasize this area in the specific recommendations that follow. In addition, because of the uncertain outlook for these preferred steps and the urgency of the situation, we offer some ''second-best'' alternatives that could be employed if the favored courses of action are not adopted.

Indeed, we applaud the adoption, on September 22, 1985, of one of those alternatives—substantial joint intervention in the exchange markets by the United States and Japan (and the other Group of Five countries). This agreement indicates a clear official recognition of the primacy of the currency

---

3. American corporate leaders deeply engaged in day-to-day business in Japan appear to recognize the primacy of these macroeconomic problems. See Herbert F. Hayde, President of Burroughs of Japan and the American Chamber of Commerce in Japan, ''US-Japan Trade Tensions: The View of American Business in Japan'' (statement before the Japan-American Society of Washington, 4 June 1985), p. 4.

problem in generating pressures for trade protection, and the need to achieve rapid adjustment of the yen/dollar rate, in particular. The initial results of the effort were encouraging, with the yen rising about 10 percent against the dollar by October 1, 1985. Continued aggressive implementation of the strategy will be needed for it to promote further correction, of course, and action on the macroeconomic fundamentals remains essential to achieve lasting equilibrium.

The United States, with its huge budget deficits, now faces a major competitive problem toward all countries because of the substantial overvaluation of the dollar. As described in chapter 2, the relative deterioration in the US trade position has been greater with many other countries than with Japan although the absolute deterioration is greatest with Japan. Japan, with declining fiscal deficits exacerbating its substantial excess of savings over investment, is running large surpluses in virtually all directions (except with countries that are mainly suppliers of primary products). Any lasting solution to the current problem, which represents the third major outbreak of US-Japan economic hostility over the past 15 years, will thus require substantial changes in exchange rates and in economic policy, particularly regarding government budgets, in both countries.

Important policy issues also arise at the structural level, both macroeconomic and microeconomic. Lasting stability in the US-Japan relationship, and hence for the world economy as a whole, may be unattainable until some fairly basic changes occur in both countries. The most pronounced structural issue is perhaps the saving-investment balance in Japan, which may require change if Japan is to avoid running sizable current account surpluses—and thus putting continuing pressure on the rest of the world. On the American side, adoption of a more determined and long-term approach by private firms may be necessary to compete effectively with the Japanese.

Philosophical and political questions obviously arise as to the propriety of one country's suggesting far-reaching changes in the underlying structure of another. However, the interdependence of today's world economy implies that deep-seated societal elements once regarded as "purely domestic" have large effects on other nations. They necessarily require delicate handling, but seem to us to be legitimate fare for international discussion.

We thus support most of the initiatives of the US government, as enumerated in chapter 1, to spur structural change in Japan that would, over time, promote greater balance in that country's international economic position. Formulation of a program for structural adjustment of depressed industries, improved financing for housing and imports, and increased flexibility for introduction of large retail chains would appear especially desirable. We are more doubtful about tax and other changes to reduce saving (although correction of the excessive incentive to saving through outright tax exemption on interest earnings would seem appropriate). The global supply of savings is sufficiently scarce that Japan's high savings rate provides a potential international social benefit, although it would be desirable to channel the available excess savings toward greater investment in Japan itself (especially the housing stock) and more investment in developing countries rather than using them to finance US fiscal deficits. Some other elements in the US proposals, such as a shortening of the Japanese work week, would probe deeply into the domestic social structure of Japan, a precedent that could later cause discomfort for the United States.

Substantial domestic forces within Japan are already seeking some of these structural changes. Indeed, one can even see the beginning of convergent attitudes in the two countries—for example, toward greater incentives for saving in the United States and greater consumption in Japan, and toward reduced scope for oligopoly arrangements in Japan and greater scope for them (at least in an international context) in the United States. However, we have not been able to address most of these issues in depth in the current study and limit our specific recommendations on them to the few topics that have emerged naturally from the analyses in chapters 2 and 3. We would note, however, that structural change is inherently long term and is thus unlikely to occur rapidly enough to defuse the present tension.

We also largely support the efforts underway by both governments to deal with the microeconomic and sector-specific problems. (As noted in chapter 3, some of these problems derive from private-sector phenomena outside at least the immediate control of government—and thus fall more into the structural than policy category.) Again, in-depth analysis of the entire range of alleged sector problems goes far beyond the scope of this (or probably any other) study, and we thus offer only a few specific proposals. We would, however, stress the urgency of moving as far and as fast as possible in these areas in an effort to defuse the pressure for extreme, and extremely costly, policy reactions, though again noting the insufficiency of even the most far-reaching actions at the sector-specific level in reducing the aggregate imbalances faced by the two countries.

Based on these conclusions, we recommend that the United States and Japan adopt a series of additional policy measures to try to defuse the current crisis. Successful resolution of the problem will require further action by both countries. The United States, in particular, with its overriding responsibilities for global economic stability, must assure a substantial correction of the exchange rate of the dollar and put its fiscal house in order. Japan, as the second largest economy in the world and perhaps the major beneficiary of an open trading system, must alter its fiscal policy substantially and go the extra mile to deal with the criticisms so widely leveled against its trade policies. The actions of both countries will have to occur at both the macroeconomic level and (especially in Japan) at the sector-specific level.

The objective of our proposed package is to reduce the current US-Japan imbalance, running at about $45 billion to $50 billion in 1985, at least to the "equilibrium" level of $20 billion to $25 billion as quickly as possible. Hence we are searching for a correction of about $25 billion.[4]

We believe that restoration of equilibrium in the exchange rate of the dollar will require its depreciation by 30 percent to 40 percent, on a trade-weighted basis from the level prevailing prior to the initiative launched by the Group of Five on September 22, 1985, including a move of at least 20 percent with respect to the yen.[5] On the basis of the calculations of appendix B, where we estimate that each percentage point of real depreciation in the bilateral exchange rate increases US exports to Japan by $270 million and reduces imports from Japan by $560 million, such a change should improve the US-Japan bilateral balance by an estimated $17 billion. Another $1 billion to $2 billion can be obtained by a speedup in the Japanese economy, to make up the "growth gap" through 1984 which added a like amount to the level of the imbalance on a one-shot basis (table 2.7, chapter 2). Elimination of Japanese import protection, overt and intangible, could add another $5 billion to $8 billion to the adjustment. And elimination of US export controls, notably on Alaskan oil, could contribute several billion dollars more. (Table 4.1 summarizes these objectives.)

Hence, it appears feasible to construct a policy package which would reduce the US-Japan imbalance to its "equilibrium" level, perhaps even

---

4. Elimination of the current American restraints on Japanese exports would of course *increase* the bilateral imbalance, perhaps by about $5 billion. Steps in this direction would have to be offset by other measures, primarily a further appreciation of the yen against the dollar.

5. This proposal is updated to the end of 1986 in the postscript, pp. 145. For the underlying analysis see John Williamson, *The Exchange Rate System*, POLICY ANALYSIS IN INTERNATIONAL ECONOMICS 5, 2d ed., rev. (Washington: Institute for International Economics, June 1985) and Marris, *Deficits and the Dollar*.

TABLE 4.1   **Correcting the US-Japan bilateral imbalance**

	Billion dollars
Level of 1985 imbalance	45–50
"Equilibrium" level (see text)	20–25
Needed short-term correction	
Without elimination of US import barriers	25
With elimination of US import barriers	30
Sources of correction	
Dollar depreciation relative to yen, 20 percent	17
Speedup in Japanese economic growth	1–2
Elimination of Japanese import barriers	5–8
Elimination of US export barriers	2–5
Total	25–32

with allowance for the impact of eliminating current US restraints on Japanese exports. (The larger correction will appear even more feasible to those who believe we underestimate the impact on US exports of eliminating Japan's trade barriers.) We turn now to the specific steps through which this outcome might be achieved.

A Proposed Package

First, it is essential that the United States launch a comprehensive program to assure correction of the exchange rate of the dollar. The announcements of late September 1985 marked a welcome recognition of the problem by the administration and the inauguration of direct efforts in the exchange markets to promote the needed realignment.

But the primary requirement for fundamental adjustment remains a sizable, credible, and sustained drive to eliminate most or all of the structural component of the budget deficit by 1988. Only by thus reducing the government's ongoing demands on the economy, leading to an excess of spending over production, and an excess of investment over saving (because of the large government dissaving) can America's external (and internal) accounts be moved toward fundamental equilibrium. The United States has repeatedly pledged in international forums, including in numerous bilateral agreements with Japan, to take such steps as its major contribution to the restoration of equilibrium; its failure to do so represents at least as great a violation of international compacts as any failure by Japan to open its markets more completely.

The budget resolution pending before the Congress at this writing (late September 1985) makes some progress in the needed direction.[6] However, independent analysis of that resolution suggests that it incorporates net reductions in the deficit of only about $30 billion to $40 billion for the current fiscal year (1986) and around $70 billion by FY 1988.[7] This would leave the deficit near $200 billion for FY 1986 and in the range of $175 billion to $200 billion for the succeeding two years, even if the resolution were to be faithfully implemented in the individual appropriations bills and the deficit were not exacerbated by a recession during this period.

Hence, substantial further action is needed to mount a convincing attack on the budget deficit. This effort will almost certainly require new tax increases as well as further cuts in nondefense spending and a slowdown in the growth of defense expenditures. Both the administration and the Congress will have to compromise on the positions they have taken to date to achieve a package of adequate size and political feasibility.

However, even a convincing attack on the budget deficit might not suffice to promote the needed dollar correction immediately. Over time, budget restraint would clearly produce lower US interest rates and a lower dollar. But by bolstering foreign confidence in the US economic outlook, serious action on the budget deficit could even propel the dollar upward in the short run and intensify the external problem.

The Federal Reserve should thus take advantage of any substantial move toward budget tightening, with its real and psychological effects in slowing inflation (and economic growth) even further, to ease monetary policy and

---

6. Congressional Budget Office, *The Economic and Budget Outlook: An Update* (Washington, August 1985).

7. James Capra and Allen Sinai, "Deficit Prospects—Half Empty or Half Full?" *Economic Study Series,* no. 14 (New York: Shearson Lehman Brothers, 1985), especially pp. 10–12.

to let it be known that it would be doing so. Even in the absence of added fiscal action, however, the Fed should now push interest rates down. With the economy soft and inflation well under control, there is little risk in such easing. Indeed, domestic conditions alone, including the fragility of the financial system, argue for such action. The rapid growth of M1 in recent months need not be a deterrent, given the sharp decline in the velocity (turnover) of money and resultant lack of meaning of that number.

Administration, congressional, and Fed leaders should also promote the needed currency change by continuing to make clear publicly, as the administration did on September 22, 1985, that they *want* to see a correction of the exchange rate for the dollar. Leading cabinet officials, notably Secretaries Baker and Baldridge, had already made numerous such statements in recent months.[8] However, President Reagan has until quite recently continued to extol the strong dollar and Federal Reserve Board Chairman Paul A. Volcker expressed concern in July over the dollar's decline at that time despite the absence of any signs of a "hard landing" or precipitous further fall. The communiqué issued in New York on September 22 by the Group of Five marked an important step toward official recognition of the need for dollar correction, but consistent and forceful follow-up is needed to convince the markets of such a change in official US intentions.

Second, Japan should reinforce the effort to correct the dollar, and move simultaneously to reduce its own current account surplus, by taking new steps to promote expanded private and public investment through tax cuts and other supply-side measures. More rapid Japanese economic growth would reduce its external surpluses both directly, by generating increased imports and lower exports (as domestic output turned more toward meeting domestic demand), and indirectly, by attracting greater capital inflows and thereby strengthening the yen. Achieving such growth through a combination of increased investment, both private and public, and a higher budget deficit would reduce the saving-investment imbalance and thereby limit net exports of both goods and capital. Like the US budget cuts, these expansionary measures in Japan should amount to perhaps 3 percent of GNP.[9]

---

8. See, for example, "Baker Calls Dollar's Decline Encouraging," *Washington Post,* 26 July 1985, and "Baldridge Sets a Dollar Goal," *New York Times,* 19 July 1985.
9. As developed in Marris, *Deficits and the Dollar,* chapter 6.

For example, Japan could stimulate spending on housing and other social infrastructure, which is recognized by most Japanese as woefully inadequate.[10] One way to do so would be to allow tax deductibility for mortgage interest payments, which could be made fiscally neutral (and simultaneously help discourage excess saving) by coupling it with increased taxation of interest earnings. This combination of steps could substantially reduce Japan's excess of savings over domestic investment. These measures would thus cut capital outflow from Japan and strengthen the yen. By increasing the after-tax profitability of yen assets, investment-oriented tax cuts (perhaps along the lines of the US investment tax credit and accelerated depreciation provision) should keep Japanese funds at home and attract more foreign capital—and thus also have a favorable direct impact on the exchange rate.

Macroeconomic steps along these lines, by both the United States and Japan, are ultimately essential if lasting correction of their external imbalances is to be achieved. Lip service has been paid to such steps in the ongoing dialogue between the two countries, but the focus of those negotiations has been on much less central issues: financial liberalization in Japan, sector-specific trade liberalization there, unitary taxation in the United States. There are obvious domestic political difficulties in dealing constructively with the macroeconomic problems in both countries, and thus considerable frustration in attempting to address them through international discussions. But there is no substitute for resolving these issues, and they should be placed at the center of all future efforts.

At the same time, there is little sign of early action of the needed magnitude on the macroeconomic front in either country. Because the urgency of reducing the external imbalances is so great, it may be necessary to pursue "second-best" strategies. This essentially means direct action on the exchange rate itself, via intervention, or on the capital flows which are the proximate source of the huge currency imbalances.

Third, once the currencies are moving in the right direction, due to other policy efforts or simply as a result of changes in market sentiment, the United States and Japan (along with the key European countries) can promote the needed correction by intervening jointly in the foreign exchange markets. Such "leaning with the wind," in the direction of both current market

---

10. As in the report to Prime Minister Nakasone of the (Okita) Advisory Committee for External Economic Relations, 9 April 1985, especially p. 15.

sentiment and underlying equilibrium, can help convince private markets of the commitment of the authorities to correct the existing misalignment and might not require the actual infusion of very large resources.[11]

Indeed, such an initiative can make credible the proposed statements of intent to correct the currency imbalance. It reduces the risk that the markets would once again reverse themselves and push the dollar back up, as occurred on at least four occasions during the rise of the dollar from mid-1980 until early 1985. From the standpoint of the United States, intervention to support the needed correction of the dollar would produce an accumulation of yen and other foreign currencies which could subsequently be used, if necessary, to slow the pace of the dollar's decline and limit the risk of overshooting in the opposite direction.

The joint intervention launched on September 22, 1985, sought to take advantage of both the medium-term decline of the dollar from late February 1985 and the immediate fall of the preceding few days. It thus seems to have a reasonable chance for success if implemented fully and credibly, and subsequently supported by actions on the fundamentals.

Another "second-best" possibility is for the Government of Japan to launch a program of substantial borrowing abroad. The proceeds from such "Nakasone bonds" would be converted into yen to strengthen its exchange rate. A similar program of "Carter bonds" was part of the successful US effort to stabilize the dollar in 1978–79. The Japanese Diet took action in 1984 to authorize such borrowing by the government.

The Japanese government would have to pay higher interest rates to borrow abroad, but could employ currency and interest-rate swaps to lower those costs (as the Japan Development Bank did on its borrowing of $100 million in early 1984). In any event, it should experience substantial capital gains from yen appreciation (as the United States did in the case of the "Carter bonds") which would be more than offsetting.

The more substantial objection to such action is that it would tend to push American interest rates up and Japanese interest rates down. A risk of such effects is inherent in any correction of the currency imbalance because it could accompany any reduction, let alone reversal, of capital flows. In

---

11. For details see C. Fred Bergsten, "The Case for Leaning with the Wind," *Financial Times,* 24 October 1984, p. 19, and Takashi Hosomi and Mitsuhiro Fukao, *A Second Look at Foreign Exchange Market Interventions* (Tokyo: Japan Center for International Finance, April 1985).

absolute terms, however, such effects could be offset ("sterilized") by modest alterations in monetary policy in the two countries and, as noted above, further easing of US monetary policy is already a desirable part of the overall policy package. If the actions were taken in the near future, there might not be much upward pressure on actual interest rates in the United States because of the softness of the economy and the related sluggishness of loan demand.

To add further to the prospects for increased capital inflow, Japan should also continue to move as rapidly as possible to modernize the Tokyo money market and thus encourage increased international use of the yen.

If necessary, Japan could also promote correction of the yen/dollar rate by limiting for a temporary period its huge capital outflows (which were running at more than $8 billion *per month* during the summer of 1985) by either a direct tax on interest earnings abroad or, more likely, by traditional "administrative guidance." Prime Minister Nakasone reportedly asked the Ministry of Finance to develop such measures in September, and Liberal Democratic Party (LDP) Vice President Nikkaido has publicly advocated such an effort.[12]

Japan currently places "prudential" limits on the outflow of capital by insurance companies and pension trusts: aggregate foreign holdings are limited to 10 percent of total portfolios, and no more than 20 percent of monthly additions to the portfolio can be placed abroad. In addition, the current rules permit very little foreign investment by the postal savings system (with yen assets in excess of the equivalent of $300 billion).

At the end of March 1985, pension trusts' holdings of foreign-currency-denominated securities had reached 8.3 percent of total assets and the five top life insurance funds were at 9.1 percent. Since total assets are growing at well over 15 percent a year, Japan will shortly be able to cut capital outflow by these institutions simply by maintaining the current limits rather than yielding to the growing pressures to relax them (and, in the case of postal savings, to permit substantial international diversification for the first time). One important loophole in these limitations could be closed, however: foreign-currency securities issued by *Japanese* companies (Sushi bonds) do not count against the ceilings.[13]

---

12. *Japan Economic Journal*, 21 September 1985, pp. 1, 3. This same issue carries a report of a proposal by the President of Nomura Securities Co. "that Japan offer $10 billion-worth of 'Nakasone bonds' in New York to correct the depreciation of the yen against the dollar."

13. See *Nomura Investment Review*, June 1985, p. 15.

The United States adopted both an Interest Equalization Tax on capital outflows, and "voluntary restraints" on outflows by banks and firms, when facing problems in the 1960s similar to those confronting Japan today: a current account surplus exceeded by net capital outflows due largely to higher interest rates abroad. There would clearly be some leakage, in light of the vastness and sophistication of today's international capital markets. Moreover, the power of the Ministry of Finance to exercise effective guidance has diminished substantially with the liberalization of Japan's capital markets since 1980, as nonfinancial institutions and wealthy individuals have become important sources of capital outflow. Nevertheless, such measures could sharply reduce Japanese investment abroad and thus substantially strengthen the yen in the exchange markets for a period.

The United States could take several steps to reinforce any such efforts by Japan to alter temporarily the international flow of capital. It could restore the withholding tax on interest earned by foreign investors in Treasury securities, perhaps at a higher level than the previous 30 percent. The Treasury could stop "tailoring" its securities to foreign tastes, reducing the incentive to invest in these "Sprinkel bonds" (as they are called in Japan) and cutting modestly into the capital inflow which props the dollar at uncompetitive levels. The United States would, of course, have to express its support for any new Japanese steps regarding capital flows. The Japanese are justifiably confused because the Treasury Department and financial community keep pressing them to liberalize more, while the interests of US business and the Congress call for action in the opposite direction.[14]

Fourth, turning to the sector-specific issues, Japan must implement fully and credibly the market-opening package originally announced by Prime Minister Nakasone on April 9, 1985. The Market-Oriented Sector-Specific (MOSS) talks must be brought to a successful conclusion. Many of the details of these programs remain to be filled in, and concrete results defined as substantially higher sales of the products covered are imperative. Specific purchases of American products should be included in the package to the greatest extent possible.

---

14. In principle, the United States could act comprehensively to limit capital inflows by taxing them or, with regard to bank deposits, by applying negative interest rates and levying special deposit requirements. The Federal Reserve did in fact take some steps in this direction in the late 1960s, when inflows from the Euromarkets were viewed as undermining its efforts to tighten domestic monetary policy. However, the dollar market is now so vast that doing so would be virtually impossible without comprehensive exchange controls.

For its part, the United States should end the embargo on exports of Alaskan oil. This would enable Japan to buy sizable quantities here and thus reduce the politically sensitive bilateral imbalance by a substantial amount (though not, by very much, the economically more important global imbalances).

Effective implementation of these sector-specific measures could make a meaningful, if modest, contribution to reducing the overall imbalance between the two countries. Moreover, to preserve a basically open trading system, it is essential for Japan to demonstrate that it recognizes the problems caused by its remaining trade barriers and is determined to take action to eliminate them. From an American perspective, it is also crucial to demonstrate that its negotiators can and will defend legitimate American trade interests. Congressional pressure to erect new barriers, in retaliation against perceived Japanese unfairness, cannot be quelled without substantial action on the sector-specific as well as macroeconomic issues.

Fifth, in addition, President Reagan and Prime Minister Nakasone need to maintain their effort to win global agreement to launch new international trade negotiations in 1986. Since the Bonn summit in May 1985 failed to set a starting date, it is particularly important for the United States and Japan to assure that the agreed preparatory talks lead to substantive negotiations next year among all members of the General Agreement on Tariffs and Trade (GATT).

The history of trade policy shows that forward movement toward new liberalization is necessary to hold off the omnipresent pressures to backslide into protectionism, particularly at a time when currency values are grossly distorted. It is particularly appropriate that Japan, in light of its huge surplus and crucial dependence on an open trading system, take a leading role in seeking international agreement to begin such negotiations. To that end, Japan, to its credit, has already decided to make a substantial "down payment" through unilateral elimination of some tariffs and reductions of 20 percent in others, as announced on June 25, and has offered to eliminate all its tariffs in the course of the negotiations.[15]

---

15. Such "down payments" by Japan would be consistent with the principle that, in implementing a general and reciprocal liberalization of trade barriers, countries with large current account surpluses should phase in their concessions first. Such an approach is advocated by Gary Clyde Hufbauer and Jeffrey J. Schott, *Trading for Growth: The Next Round of Trade Negotiations,* POLICY ANALYSES IN INTERNATIONAL ECONOMICS 11 (Washington: Institute for International Economics, September 1985).

Sixth, the United States and Japan should also jointly initiate an effort to achieve basic improvements in the international monetary system. This study has concluded that currency misalignments have been the major source of escalation of economic tension between the two countries during the past 15 years. These exchange rate problems have arisen under both fixed and flexible exchange rates. Hence, it would greatly behoove the two countries to launch serious negotiations to find a better international monetary mechanism, which would help avoid such severe periodic imbalances between them.

The report issued by the Deputies of the Group of Ten in Tokyo in June 1985 in fact recognized the shortcomings of the present monetary regime, noting explicitly that it "failed to promote sound national policies." That report, however, despite recording a minority view to the contrary, rejected the most promising way to remedy the problems it identified: adoption of a "target zone" approach to currency management.

Under such a system, the major countries would first agree on the criteria that should guide relationships among their currencies—basically, the achievement over time of current account balances consistent with sustainable levels of international capital flow. They would then apply these criteria to current exchange rate relationships, defining zones of 15 percent to 20 percent within which they would pledge to maintain those relationships. The zones would in fact "crawl" over time, as underlying economic conditions shifted, to permit the needed dynamics for the system. Indeed, such an approach could readily be incorporated within the decision of the Group of Ten to enhance the international surveillance mechanism of the International Monetary Fund by providing objective benchmarks against which the international compatibility of national policies and economic performance could be judged.[16]

What Not to Do

It is also essential to indicate what should *not* be done to deal with the US-Japan trade problem: neither country should resort to new trade controls in an effort to resolve the current difficulties or even to buy time for their lasting solution. As indicated throughout this study, trade *policy* can have relatively little impact on the trade *deficit*—which is primarily a function of

---

16. Details can be found in Williamson, *The Exchange Rate System.*

exchange rate and macroeconomic factors. Unfortunately, initiatives to apply sweeping new trade measures abound in both countries in a misguided (or disingenuous) effort to help correct the external imbalances. In the United States, there are numerous proposals to apply an import surcharge—for revenue as well as trade reasons—either generally or against Japan alone.[17] Likewise, there are proposals in Japan to try to deflect the problem by imposing an across-the-board export surcharge or new "voluntary" export restraints in "sensitive" sectors.

In our view, such steps would do nothing to correct the disequilibrium and might well make it worse. New Japanese export controls or an American import surcharge could be expected to produce a renewed weakening of the yen against the dollar, because of the expected reduction in the American trade deficit and Japanese trade surplus, offsetting most or all of the direct improvement in the trade balance which such steps might achieve.[18] In addition, particularly if the action were initiated from this side of the Pacific, the exercise of muscle by the United States (though soundly denounced throughout the world) could reinforce the "safe-haven" appeal of the dollar. Such moves would of course divert attention from dealing with the fundamental issues for correcting the dollar disequilibrium.[19]

Imposition of widespread import controls by the United States, including a general surcharge, could also have extremely negative effects on the world economy. Retaliation or emulation would be virtually certain from a wide range of countries, including Europe and most of the developing world. As a result, the international trading system would be disrupted severely—perhaps so much as to undermine one of the key foundations of postwar prosperity (and political harmony). If such controls applied to the developing

---

17. Such action could occur either via new legislation or by presidential action under section 122 of the Trade Act of 1974, which authorizes the President to apply a surcharge of either variety up to 15 percent for a period of 150 days, renewable with congressional approval.

18. Even serious US contemplation of added trade barriers against Japan has frequently been reported in the exchange markets as depressing the yen. Protectionist pressures, let alone actual protectionist steps, may thus backfire against their proponents by further improving the price competitiveness of Japanese products.

19. It is incorrect to argue, as some have, that the revenue effect of a US import surcharge would reduce US interest rates and thus the dollar. The surcharge is inherently a temporary device, which would therefore have no lasting impact on the fiscal imbalance and little, if any, effect on the financial markets. It is more likely that adoption of a surcharge would deflect progress toward lasting budget cuts, exacerbating rather than resolving the dollar problem.

countries, the "debt bomb" could explode as the debtors were denied the opportunity to earn the foreign exchange needed to service their external obligations.

A US import surcharge applied solely to Japan (or, like the Bentsen-Gephardt-Rostenkowski bill, only to Japan and a few others) would have fewer adverse effects on the trading system in practical terms (and, likewise, would promise much smaller reductions in US imports and gains in fiscal receipts). However, it would directly violate the most-favored-nation principle of Article I of the GATT. It could still be expected to trigger an offsetting move in the yen/dollar exchange rate, which would obviate most (or all) of its intended benefits for US trade. Moreover, such discriminatory treatment would presumably have enormous and lasting impact on overall US-Japan relations and future security relations in the Pacific—and might reduce, or even eliminate, Japanese willingness to cooperate further with the United States on economic (or other) issues.

If the trade crunch ever reached such a point that restriction became inevitable, a Japanese export surcharge might be less bad than any US action. It would avoid discrimination, with its severe foreign-policy and GATT effects; "compensate" Japan with the surcharge revenues for its cut in sales volume; and enhance the likelihood for early removal. However, effectiveness would still be an issue: the further reduction in the Japanese budget deficit, due to the surcharge revenues, would raise the Japanese savings surplus still further and promote an offsetting rise in its trade surplus.

American exporters who seek improved access to the Japanese market, or better performance against Japanese competitors in third markets, would be affected adversely by any new restraints on Japanese exports to the United States. In many cases, the costs of their inputs would be raised and their price competitiveness damaged directly. The induced rise in the dollar would price them even further out of world markets, in Japan itself and elsewhere. And, in the case of a global surcharge, direct retaliation (especially from Europe) and losses of purchasing power (especially in Latin America) would levy sizable additional costs on them.

The *threat* of a US surcharge, or even an actual US decision (by Congress or the President) to put a surcharge into effect at a specified date in the future unless Japan met explicit US trade demands, would presumably be less damaging. Indeed, many who espouse such a course freely admit that they do so in order to prod Japan to make concessions of the type discussed throughout this study (primarily at the sector-specific level), and would not really wish to see such controls put into effect. Unfortunately, the pattern of trade bargaining with Japan in the past does suggest that action is seldom forthcoming without such pressures.

The problem, of course, is that brinkmanship can easily get out of control—and the actual implementation of some of the proposed measures could clearly set back any potential improvement in US-Japan economic relations on all fronts. Moreover, we have noted throughout this analysis that structural issues will inherently take much time to change and that even the entire range of needed sector-specific changes will not much alter the overall imbalances. We are thus critical of the failure to address the most promising area for sizable medium-term payoff: macroeconomic policy in the two countries. However, *trade* policy threats are not well designed to achieve *macroeconomic* policy changes—indeed, as noted, the proponents of most such threats see them as levers to open markets for specific products or redress allegedly unfair trade practices.[20]

Less extreme suggestions (as noted in chapter 1) call for new or tightened import controls for individual industries, ranging from smokestack to high tech, and for seeking "reciprocity" in a more rigorous manner than the provisions for that purpose included in the Trade and Tariff Act of 1984. We cannot address all of these proposals in detail. Regarding the "reciprocity" bills, however, we would suggest an analogy from the history of civil rights. It is clearly impossible to legislate, or otherwise mandate, equal trade *outcomes* in a given sector for the United States and Japan (or any two countries) in each other's markets. Differences in national comparative advantage militate against any such results, except by pure coincidence.

There can be no objection to the pursuit of reciprocal *opportunities*, however, in the markets of countries at roughly similar levels of development. Indeed, as noted in chapter 3, reciprocity has been largely achieved among the major industrial countries with regard to overall levels of tariffs and, to some extent, overt nontariff barriers. The goal of aggregate reciprocity has been a guiding principle of postwar trade negotiations. Proposals for reciprocal market opportunities at the sectoral level are an extension of this concept, and should be acceptable for the same reasons. The agreement in the Tokyo Round to eliminate tariffs on aircraft is one example, and the US-Japan

---

20. To date, congressional threats of trade restrictions appear to have had their greatest impact on the Reagan administration, leading to an admission of the seriousness of dollar overvaluation and a reversal of its opposition to coordinated intervention efforts to correct the dollar.

agreement in 1983 to eliminate tariffs on semiconductors is another.[21] However, sectoral reciprocity should be pursued primarily through international negotiation and in conformity with GATT rules. Retaliatory imposition of new protection on grounds of nonreciprocity not only would violate GATT but would also risk a vicious circle of escalating retaliation, and would be especially unwarranted where the allegations of nonreciprocal treatment refer to vague impediments primarily inferred from actual outcomes. (In contrast, where identifiable barriers such as quotas and licensing exist, compensatory action under the GATT could be claimed by virtue of the country's nullification of tariff concessions through nontariff means, under GATT Article XXIII.)[22]

It is clear that a wide range of trade policy threats will continue at least until the overall imbalances being experienced by the two countries are reduced to much lower levels. Indeed, it is partly because they could spiral out of control that we propose an urgent and broadly based attack on all components of the problem. But traditional negotiating efforts, *if focused on the right* (i.e., macroeconomic policy) *issues* and offering in return meaningful US action on its macroeconomic policy problems, would seem much better designed to achieve the needed Japanese changes.

---

21. Japan Economic Institute, *Yearbook of U.S.-Japan Economic Relations in 1983* (Washington, 1984), p. 52

22. William R. Cline, *"Reciprocity": A New Approach to World Trade Policy?* POLICY ANALYSES IN INTERNATIONAL ECONOMICS 2 (Washington: Institute for International Economics, 1982), pp. 32–33. Note that there may be a special case for sectoral reciprocity in telecommunications. On both sides, recent structural changes have occurred. In the United States the breakup of AT&T probably increased the degree of market access for foreign suppliers, because AT&T had previously purchased most of its equipment from its subsidiary, Western Electric. This indirect market opening was taken without requiring any corresponding opening in the telecommunications markets of other countries. On the Japanese side, the government has recently privatized NTT, raising the possibility that this entity may now make foreign purchases that otherwise would not have occurred because of discriminatory government procurement. As noted in chapter 3, some observers expect even a private NTT to discriminate against imports. In principle, however, the recent potential opening of both markets as a result of structural change is a unique opportunity to implement sectoral reciprocity without upsetting broader reciprocal bargains obtained in earlier, across-the-board negotiations (where concessions in some sectors are often made in exchange for foreign liberalization in others). Ideally, however, such reciprocity should be obtained through negotiation (and US negotiators have already achieved considerable progress in obtaining desired changes in Japan's telecommunications sector), not by threats to close the US market. Note also that implementation of such threats would appear to impose a competitive disadvantage on US communications firms other than AT&T, by forcing them to purchase more of their equipment from Western Electric.

There is one more important role for trade policy in contributing to a solution of the US-Japan problem, in addition to the new market-opening measures and launching of international negotiations cited above. We concluded in chapter 3 that two aspects of Japan's "industry targeting," its delayed effects on trade competition and its occasional resort to "infant-industry" protection, create real problems for other countries which require effective responses. Wherever government subsidies or corporate dumping can be clearly identified and demonstrated, the United States (and other countries) should be extremely tough in applying countervailing and anti-dumping duties against them. Such responses are not "protectionist," and should have none of the adverse consequences just cited for sweeping trade barriers.

In addition, Japan (and the United States and all other advanced industrial countries) should explicitly renounce the right to apply any type of trade distortion for "infant-industry" purposes. It is simply unacceptable for the two largest and most advanced countries to utilize such devices, which should be reserved for developing countries (and, even there, carefully circumscribed to avoid abuse). Such a declaration could be an important part of the results of the proposed new round of multilateral trade negotiations, and could be adopted unilaterally by the United States and Japan much sooner.

Conclusion

The US-Japan problem has already become a major crisis for both the world economy and for overall US-Japan relations. Unfortunately, a quite plausible scenario could bring it to the point of eruption:

• The dollar remains strong, despite the actions announced in late September 1985, and the US trade deficit soars toward $150 billion in 1985 and more in 1986. Correspondingly, the Japanese surplus soars to $50 billion, and perhaps beyond.

• The American economy continues to grow slowly or even falls into recession, and the unemployment rate starts to climb, importantly because of the trade deterioration—with no possibility for responding with fiscal policy changes because the budget deficit is already so high.

• The efforts to forge a responsible budget package remain inadequate.

• Japan fails to convincingly liberalize its markets for imports.

In such an environment, toward the end of 1985 and particularly into 1986, real and psychological problems could push the Congress, and even the administration, toward lashing out at Japan. There would be a very real economic problem, and much of it would be due to the huge trade deficit. There would be deep frustration over the continuing inability to deal responsibly with America's own overriding domestic problem, the budget deficit, and at Japan's apparent unwillingness to shoulder responsibilities befitting the world's second largest economy. Crucial congressional elections would be looming in November 1986. The temptation to scapegoat and retaliate, perhaps by "taxing the foreigners," could be very strong—even more so than in 1971, when Richard M. Nixon and John B. Connally applied the previous US import surcharge.

Given the depth of the imbalances, it may already be too late to avert a collision. But the damage that would result could be enormous to the US economy and foreign policy, and to the world as a whole. The stakes are extremely high, and the United States and Japan should redouble their efforts to avoid the crunch.

They should seek to negotiate a multifaceted package along the lines suggested here, building on the promising start announced on September 22, 1985, for implementation on a clear timetable over the coming months. The short-run package should include extensive joint intervention, a further easing of US monetary policy and perhaps some direct manipulation of capital flows (mainly via Japanese borrowing abroad and administrative guidance on outflows), and substantial further liberalization of trade flows. For the medium run, both countries need to alter the direction of their fiscal policies. Over the longer haul, structural changes are in order—both within the two countries, regarding the Japanese saving-investment balance and American firms' efforts to penetrate the Japanese market, and to reform the international trade and monetary systems. Such a comprehensive effort is essential to resolve the enormous problems caused for both countries by the trade imbalance and to avoid a potentially disastrous disruption of both the world economy and overall relationships in the Pacific.

5   Postscript

Three developments since the first edition of this volume in October 1985 have significantly affected our conclusions and recommendations, and call for comment in this second edition. They are the sharp decline in the world price of oil with its substantial impact on the equilibrium exchange rate relationship between the dollar and the yen, the likely impact on the United States–Japan trade imbalance of the large change in the yen-dollar exchange rate that has now taken place, and the United States–Japan agreement of October 31, 1986, with its potentially significant implications for managing the economic relationship between the two countries.

The Equilibrium Exchange Rate

Between late 1985 and the end of 1986, the world price of oil declined by an amount roughly equal to its increase in 1979–80 ("the second oil shock"). Because Japan is much more dependent on imported oil than most other countries, including the United States, this change has an important impact on the fundamental equilibrium exchange rate for the yen and the bilateral equilibrium rate between the dollar and the yen. Our colleague John Williamson has noted that the rise in the oil price from 1978 to 1980 required a yen depreciation of about 15 percent.[1] Hence, the reversal of the oil price by a like magnitude in 1985–86 suggests the need for a similar appreciation of the yen.

We concluded in chapter 4 that the equilibrium yen-dollar rate as of mid-

---

1. John Williamson, *The Exchange Rate System*, POLICY ANALYSES IN INTERNATIONAL ECONOMICS 5, Washington: Institute for International Economics, June 1985 rev., pp. 30–31, based on estimates by Anne Kenny McGuirk, "Oil Price Changes and Real Exchange Rate Movements Among Industrial Countries," *IMF Staff Papers*, December 1983.

1985 was about 190:1. Adjusting by 15 percent for the fall in world oil prices would shift the equilibrium rate at the present time to about 160:1.[2]

In addition, over time the yen will probably have to appreciate steadily against the dollar for three reasons. The first is the prospect for continuing higher productivity growth in Japan than in the United States, especially in the tradable goods sector.[3] The second is the outlook for continuing lower inflation in Japan than in the United States. Third is the growing surplus of investment income in Japan, which has become the world's largest creditor country, contrasted with the declining investment income position of the United States as it has become the world's largest debtor country.

These three factors might support an average annual appreciation of the yen against the dollar of 4 percent or 5 percent. If so, and in view of the impact of lower world oil prices, the equilibrium yen-dollar rate might have approximated 150:1 by the end of 1986 and could move to between 140:1 and 145:1 in 1987.[4]

Currency Changes Since 1985 and the Trade Imbalances

The second major development concerning the United States–Japan economic problem since we published this study is, of course, the substantial depreciation of the dollar against most other major currencies, including the yen. The yen-dollar rate rose to almost 150:1 in early September 1986 and, after falling back to almost 165:1, has again appreciated beyond 160:1 at this writing. The rate has thus come quite close to the level recommended in this study, adjusted per the previous paragraphs.

---

2. This recalculation was first suggested in C. Fred Bergsten, "The United States–Japan Economic Problem: The G-5 Plaza Agreement After Six Months" (address to the Japan Society, New York, NY, 12 March 1986), pp. 6–10.

3. In Appendix B, for example, the coefficient in the US import equation for Japan's industrial output suggests that US imports from Japan would grow 2 percent a year faster than Japan's imports from the United States in the absence of further currency changes.

4. Somewhat similar views are expressed by Lawrence B. Krause, "Does a Yen Valued at 100 per Dollar Make Any Sense?" (unpublished paper, 31 January 1986) and Edward M. Bernstein, Statement to the Subcommittee on Commerce, Transportation and Tourism, House of Representatives, 25 February 1986, esp. p. 6.

Despite this sharp change in the currency relationship, the external deficit of the United States and the external surplus of Japan rose to record highs in 1986 (as foreseen on page 126). This has produced disappointment in many quarters, and doubt in some that even such large exchange rate adjustments would produce the needed reduction in the imbalances of the two countries.

Traditionally, however, it takes 12 to 18 months for a currency change to lead to an absolute improvement in trade and current account positions. This is because of the three lags which together comprise the "J curve": the lag from change in exchange rate to change in prices of traded products, the lag from this change in price to alterations in demand patterns and production runs, and the lag from changes in orders to actual shipments and inclusion in the published statistics. Hence, it should be no surprise that the imbalances of the United States and Japan actually grew from 1985 to 1986.

Moreover, there are reasons to believe that the J curve may take longer than normal to play through in the current episode. This is partly because the overvaluation of the dollar was so large (40 percent to 50 percent at its peak in early 1985) that foreign exporters built enormous profit margins and thus did not have to respond to the currency change by altering prices until that change had gone quite far. In addition, the dollar remained substantially overvalued for so long (at least four years) that many foreign firms committed considerable investments to entering the American market, and it may thus take more than just a reversal of the dollar's climb to dislodge them in the future. For similar reasons, some American exporters may have become so demoralized by being priced out of world markets for so long that it will take them a good deal of time to rebuild their marketing efforts abroad and to take advantage of the renewed price competitiveness of the dollar.

In any event, the J curve in the current episode should be dated only from late 1985 or even early 1986. The dollar began its decline against most major currencies, including the yen, in February or March 1985. But most economic agents around the world concluded that the exchange rates were changing sizably and "permanently" only after the Plaza Agreement of September 1985 was viewed as succeeding in correcting the prolonged misalignment. Even with normal lags, we should therefore not have expected to see an absolute decline in the international imbalances until the end of 1986 and, more likely, into 1987.

We therefore remain confident that the currency changes now achieved, assuming that they are not wholly or largely reversed, will lead to a substantial reduction in the bilateral imbalance between the United States and Japan (as well as in the global imbalances of the two countries). Indeed, the volume of Japanese exports has already turned down sharply enough to substantially slow the growth of that entire economy, and the prices of American imports from Japan have risen considerably. We anticipate that a good deal of recorded improvement in trade balances will occur in 1987 with further gains in 1988. Since the decline of the dollar against the yen has been over 30 percent, the parameters developed in chapter 4 and Appendix B—updated to the 1986 base values of imports from Japan of approximately $87 billion and a bilateral deficit of approximately $60 billion—suggest the amount of the reduction could be some $30 billion, bringing the bilateral deficit relatively close to the structural equilibrium identified in chapter 2.

The United States–Japan Agreement of October 1986

One of the recommendations in this study is that the United States and Japan "jointly institute an effort to achieve basic improvements in the international monetary system" (page 138). We suggested that a target-zone approach to currency management might be the most promising avenue for such reform.

The United States and Japan appear to have taken a step in this direction with their agreement of October 31, 1986. That agreement records *inter alia* the view that "the exchange rate realignment achieved between the yen and the dollar since the Plaza Agreement is now broadly consistent with the present underlying economic fundamentals."[5] In explaining the agreement, a senior Treasury official on the same day twice called attention to the fact that the yen-dollar rate was "at the low end of its recent trading range against the dollar, i.e., the trading range that has (existed) during the discussions on this agreement" from early September 1986 until October 31. He quantified this range as "between its present level (about 164:1) and 151:1, 152:1, 153:1, somewhere in there."[6]

It therefore seems reasonable to interpret this arrangement as a tentative

---

5. Agreement between the United States and Japan on Cooperative Action and Understandings Regarding a Number of Economic Issues of Mutual Concern, 31 October 1986, p. 2.

6. Such a range would envisage a slightly weaker rate for the yen than suggested by our updated analysis as presented here, which would center on a rate of 150:1 and might thus range between 135:1 and 165:1.

first step toward the development of a target zone for the dollar-yen relationship. The two countries have not made an official declaration of the rates which border the zone nor have they announced any new policy commitments, so it remains to be seen what impact and duration the agreement will have.[7] But we regard it as a significant effort to help avoid renewed misalignment of the dollar-yen relationship, and hope that the two countries will build on it in constructive ways in the months and years ahead.

---

7. Indeed, the arrangement falls far short of a true target zone regime as developed in Williamson, *The Exchange Rate System,* pp. 62–72 and 85–90. This author favors public announcement of the zones; calls for national commitments to adjust interest rates to defend the zones if necessary; envisages their adoption by at least three countries to truly constitute a new ''system''; and advocates a wider zone (between 15 percent and 20 percent) than that implied by the Treasury statement (about 10 percent).

Appendices

A Structural Bilateral Deficit as a Function of Japan's Current Account Surplus

Let x = the ratio of Japan's exports to GNP; m = the ratio of its imports to GNP; s = the ratio of its balance on services and transfers to GNP; and c = the ratio of the current account balance to GNP. Then:

(1) $x - m + s = c.$

Suppose that for any given increase in Japan's current account and trade balances, two-thirds occurs through increased exports and one-third through a reduction in imports. Using subscript o to denote values in the base case,

(2) $x = x_o + 0.67(c - c_o).$

If the balance on services typically stands at a given fraction, a, of trade turnover,

(3) $s = a(x + m).$

Given the parameter a and the base values x_o and c_o, then for any postulated current account surplus as a fraction of GNP, c, find x and m. To facilitate the calculation, define h as the ratio of imports to exports, or $h = m/x$. Then:

(4) $x - hx + a(x + hx) = c,$

$$\text{or}$$

(4') $x(1 - h + a + ah) = c.$

Incorporating equation (2), the ratio of exports to imports at the specified current account surplus relative to GNP must be:

(5) $h = -\dfrac{\{c/[x_o + 0.67(c - c_o)]\} - 1 - a.}{1 + a}$

Given x (from equation 2) and h (equation 5), m *equals hx.* The trade balance as a fraction of GNP is $x - m$. Bilateral trade with the United States, as a fraction of Japan's GNP, is: $x_u = kx$; $m_u = rm$, where x_u is Japan's exports to the United States and m_u is its imports from the United

States (as a fraction of Japan's GNP); k and r are trade pattern coefficients. The bilateral trade balance as a fraction of Japan's GNP thus *equals* $x_u -m_u$.

This model is applied to estimated 1984 GNP for Japan of \$1,223 billion. The parameters used are: $k = 0.261$; $r = 0.183$; $c_o = 0.0181$; $x_o = 0.127$. The US trade coefficients (k, r) are based on 1977–83 averages; the initial ratios of exports (x_o) and current account (c_o) to GNP are from a 1983 base. The services parameter (a) was -0.047 in the period 1977–83 but is assumed to be zero in the future. Data are from text table 2.3 and from *International Financial Statistics*.

B A Model of US–Japan Trade

Diagnosis of the causes of the rising US trade deficit with Japan requires a quantitative model that explains trade between the two countries. This appendix develops such a model on the basis of statistically estimated trade equations.

On the side of US imports from Japan, an important influence is the price of imports from Japan relative to the price of domestic US substitutes. The lower this relative price, the greater the incentive to import. The import price in dollar terms is affected by the yen-dollar exchange rate and the rate of domestic inflation in Japan; the price relative to US prices is also influenced by the rate of domestic US inflation. In broad terms, a sharp rise in the number of yen per dollar from 1980 to 1984 accompanied by lower inflation in Japan than in the United States meant a reduction in the dollar price of imports from Japan relative to US prices of competing goods, causing a rise in imports.

Income also influences import demand, in two ways. First, there is the long-term growth in import demand associated with steady income growth, or the "secular" income influence. Second, there is a cyclical income influence as well. Because of inventory variation and such factors as the tendency to use imports for marginal supply, the sensitivity of imports to a cyclical change in the domestic economy can substantially exceed what would be predicted on a basis of the long-term trend relating imports to income.

There are also important influences on the supply side of imports. In the case of Japan, rapidly outward-shifting supply associated with technological progress appears to have been a significant factor in expansion of exports to the United States and other countries.[1] In addition, the cyclical state of the

---

1. In terms of supply and demand diagrams, this influence may be seen as an outward shift of the Japanese supply curve, while the expansion of the market associated with US income growth represents an outward shift of the demand curve.

Japanese economy may be expected to influence supply of US imports from Japan. When the Japanese economy is slack, greater supply of exports to the United States will be available than when the Japanese economy is operating at full capacity and Japanese firms tend to push their export activities harder.

Finally, the cross-exchange rate between Japan and other industrial countries should influence Japan's share in total US imports. When the yen is weak relative to the deutsche mark and other major currencies, imports from Japan will tend to rise relative to those from other industrial countries.

On the side of US exports to Japan, the same variables (economic influences) are likely to explain trade. US exports will depend on the price of US goods relative to those in Japan, on the level of income in Japan, the cyclical state of the Japanese and US economies, and the exchange rate of the dollar relative to the currencies of competing countries.

The existing quantitative literature on US-Japanese trade provides a point of departure for a quantitative model along these lines. An exhaustive econometric study by Peter A. Petri provides perhaps the most reliable estimate for one of the key building blocks of a quantitative model: the elasticity, or responsiveness, of US imports from Japan (in quantity terms) to the change in the price of imports. Petri estimates this price elasticity at -2.12. This estimate indicates that a 1 percent increase in the price of imports from Japan causes a 2.1 percent reduction in the quantity of imports. Furthermore, he finds that the best statistical results are obtained by incorporating a weight of 0.6 on the current year influence of import prices, 0.3 on the price lagged one year, and 0.1 on the price lagged two years. Petri reports estimates of the import price elasticity from other authors, and shows that his estimate is centrally located in the range of existing estimates.[2]

Because Petri's statistical relationship is estimated using a supply-shares approach (considering the share of supply to the US market provided by US, Japanese, and other producers), it does not contain a direct estimate of the secular and cyclical income elasticities. To incorporate these variables as well as the others enumerated above into the model, it is possible to develop a statistical equation that constrains the import price elasticity to the result found by Petri, and directly estimates the elasticities for the other independent variables.

---

2. Peter A. Petri, *Modeling Japanese–American Trade: A Study of Asymmetric Interdependence* (Cambridge, Mass.: Harvard University Press, 1984), pp. 52–71.

The basic form of the import function outlined above is:

(1) $M_t^q = KP_t^b P_{t-1}^c Y_{U,t}^d A_{U,t}^f A_{J,t}^g C_t^h Z_t^k,$

where M_t^q is the quantity of US imports from Japan, t refers to the current year and $t - 1$ to the prior year, P is the price of imports relative to domestic US prices, Y is US real GNP, A is the ratio of actual GNP to trend GNP (a measure of cyclical status of the economy), C is industrial capacity in Japan, and Z is an index of the real yen exchange rate relative to currencies of other (non-US) industrial countries. Subscripts U and J refer to the United States and Japan, respectively, and the superscripts on variables on the right-hand side of the equation refer to elasticities.

In a regression equation incorporating an imposed value on one of the coefficients, the dependent variable becomes the original dependent variable as transformed by the independent variables for which the constrained parameter values are known. For purposes of estimating the elasticities other than the (constrained) price elasticity, the dependent variable M_t^q may be transformed by dividing by the price terms on the right-hand side of (1), giving:

(1a) $M_t' = M_t^q / [P_t^b P_{t-1}^c] = K Y_t^d A_{U,t}^f A_{J,t}^g C_t^h Z_t^k.$

Here, the known parameters b and c *equal* -1.272 and -0.848, respectively, or 0.6 and 0.4 *times* the composite price elasticity of -2.12 (following Petri's lag structure).

Estimation of (1a) in logarithmic form yields the following results:[3]

(1b) $\log M_t' = -0.858 + 0.679 \log Y_t + 1.622 \log A_{U,t}$
$\qquad\qquad$ (0.22)   (1.45)$\qquad\qquad$ (2.25)

$\qquad\qquad\quad -1.686 \log A_{J,t} + 1.148 \log C_t + 0.147 \log Z_t,$
$\qquad\qquad\quad$ (2.58)$\qquad\qquad$ (6.10)$\qquad\qquad$ (0.40)

$\qquad\qquad\quad \bar{R}^2 = 0.9877; DW = 1.88.$

Figures shown in parentheses are t-statistics. The other test statistics are overall degree of explanation adjusted for degrees of freedom ($\bar{R}^2$) and Durbin–Watson statistic (DW). Equation (1b) is estimated using annual data

---

3. Note that because of the relatively small number of observations (24), when the full model was estimated directly, including the current and lagged import price, the activity variables lost statistical significance. Superior statistical results were obtained by using the constrained Petri import price elasticities and estimating the remaining parameters by the method shown here.

for 1960 to 1984.[4] In the equation, "log" refers to the natural logarithm. The components of the transformed import variable, M'_t, are as follows. Real imports, Mq_t, *equal* the dollar value of US imports from Japan *divided by* the index of dollar prices of Japan's exports. (Note that the Japanese export price index is more reliable than most because it is a special index of actual export prices rather than a unit value index obtained by dividing export values by export quantities.) Originally in terms of yen, the export price index is converted to a dollar basis using the average exchange rate for the year. The relative price of imports, P_t, with its current and lagged values appropriately divided into Mq_t to obtain M'_t in the particular specification noted above, *equals* the dollar price index of Japanese exports *divided by* the US wholesale price index (to deflate for general US inflation).

The index of industrial capacity in Japan *equals* the index of actual industrial production or the previous peak of this index, whichever is higher. The cross-exchange rate Z is a real index (deflating by wholesale prices within Japan and other countries) of the rate of exchange between the yen and other (non-US) currencies, weighting by shares of these countries in US imports. (A higher value of Z indicates more real yen per real unit of other currencies, and thus depreciation of the yen relative to them.) The trend lines for US and Japanese real GNP used to estimate the term A for each country are obtained by regression estimates of logistics curves, in which the percentage change of GNP *equals* a constant *plus* a (negative) coefficient *times* the level of GNP.

The estimates in equation (1b) are strong in statistical terms. Adjusting for degrees of freedom, 99 percent of the variation of the dependent variable is explained by the equation ($\bar{R}^2$). All variables have the correct signs. Statistical significance as measured by the t-statistic (in parentheses) is high for both of the cyclical income variables (above the 5 percent level) and the Japanese industrial capacity variable (above the 1 percent level), although the current income variable is significant only at the 15 percent level. The cross-exchange rate variable is not statistically significant. The estimates indicate that a 1 percent increase in US income on a long-term basis causes an increase of 0.68 percent in imports from Japan; a 1 percent cyclical upswing in US income causes an increase in imports of 1.62 percent; a 1 percent cyclical upswing in Japan reduces US imports by 1.69 percent; and

---

4. Data for the estimates are primarily from IMF, *International Financial Statistics*, various issues, and *Direction of Trade Statistics Yearbook 1985*. The wholesale price index for manufactures in Japan, cited below, is from the Morgan Guaranty data bank.

a 1 percent rise in long-term industrial capacity in Japan increases US imports by 1.15 percent. Implications of these parameters are considered further below.

Given these estimates, the consolidated equation for use in simulating US imports from Japan (for the analysis in chapter 2) is:

(1c) $M_t^q = e^{-0.858} P_t^{-1.272} P_{t-1}^{-0.848} Y_t^{0.679} A_{U,t}^{1.622} A_{J,t}^{-1.686} C_t^{1.148} Z_t^{0.147}$.

This equation states imports in quantity terms (in dollar values at 1980 prices). To obtain imports in current dollar terms, it is necessary to incorporate the impact of the exchange rate change on dollar prices of Japan's exports. That is, when the number of dollars per yen increases by, for example, 10 percent (dollar depreciation), the dollar price of Japan's exports will rise by 10 percent *minus* some amount representing the portion of the depreciation which exporters do not "pass through" to their prices. This price relationship is estimated as follows:

(2) $\dot{p}_{J,t}^x = -0.881 + 0.862 \, \dot{p}_{J,t}^d + 0.738 \, \dot{R}_{DPY,t}$
            (1.4)   (11.2)   (10.7)

            $\bar{R}^2 = 0.9051; DW = 2.02,$

where $\dot{p}_{J,t}^x$ is the percentage change in Japan's dollar export prices, $\dot{p}_{J,t}^d$ is the percentage change in Japan's domestic wholesale price index for manufactures, and $\dot{R}_{DPY,t}$ is the percentage change in the nominal exchange rate (defined as dollars per yen). (The estimation period is 1960–84.) These results, also highly significant in statistical terms, indicate that a 10 percent depreciation of the dollar causes dollar prices of Japanese exports to rise by 7.4 percent, meaning a pass-through ratio of three-quarters.

Equations (1c) and (2) are then used as the basis for estimating the current dollar value of US imports from Japan, as follows:

(2a) $P_{m,t} = P_{m,t-1}(1 + \dot{p}_{J,t}^x); M_t^V = P_{m,t} M_t^q,$

where $P_{m,t}$ is the import price in year t, and M_t^V is import value in current dollars.

Equations (1c), (2), and (2a) are thus combined to obtain the current dollar value of imports under actual conditions and alternative hypothesized conditions (equilibrium exchange rate, historical average for growth differential between Japan and the United States) in the analysis of chapter 2. An important implication of the equations it that the basic conditions exist for a depreciation of the dollar to reduce not only the quantity but also the dollar value of imports from Japan. Thus, a 10 percent depreciation of the dollar relative to the yen (with domestic wholesale prices held constant in both countries) causes a 7.4 percent rise in the dollar price of imports from Japan. Applied to the elasticity of -2.12 for import volume response to the relative price of imports, the result is a decline of import volume by 15.7 percent. After taking account of the price increase of 7.4 percent, the net impact on the dollar volume of imports is a reduction of 9.4 percent ($0.843 \times 1.074 = 0.906$).

For US exports, annual data for 1960–84 yield the following equation:

$$(3) \quad \log X_t^q = -1.333 - \quad 1.159\, R^*_{YPD,t} + 0.784 \log Y_{J,t} - 0.017\, D_t$$
$$ (0.89) \qquad\quad (3.84) \qquad\quad (12.24) \qquad\quad (0.19)$$
$$+ 1.811 \log A_{J,t} - 2.195 \log A_{U,t},$$
$$ (3.38) \qquad\quad (2.82)$$
$$\overline{R}^2 = 0.9772;\, DW = 1.75.$$

Here, X_t^q is an index of real US exports to Japan, obtained by deflating the current dollar value of these exports by the index of unit values of US exports. The term $R^*_{YPD,t}$ is the real exchange rate, this time expressed in real yen per real dollar, and deflated by wholesale prices for the United States and the wholesale price index for manufactures for Japan (where the use of the overall wholesale price index could introduce greater distortion associated with the oil shocks). This real exchange rate term represents the effective price of US exports in the Japanese market. The terms for cyclical activity level (A) are as before. The dummy variable D takes the value of 1 for 1960–70 and zero thereafter, to allow for a possible shift in imports associated with market liberalization in the 1970s and after. Tests incorporating the cross-exchange rate (Z) found it insignificant, and it is omitted in (3).

Statistically, the export equation is strong. Overall explanation is 98 percent. All of the income and price terms are significant at the 1 percent level. Only the dummy variable for 1960–70 is insignificant.

The export results indicate a substantial responsiveness of US exports to the real exchange rate. A 1 percent real depreciation of the dollar increases the real volume of US exports to Japan by 1.16 percent. Similarly, the income and cyclical elasticities are substantial: a 1 percent rise in long-term Japanese GNP increases US exports to Japan by 0.78 percent; a cylical upswing in Japanese GNP by 1 percent increases US exports by 1.81 percent; and a cyclical upswing by 1 percent in the United States reduces exports by 2.20 percent.

The simulations in chapter 3 convert the physical quantum of exports predicted by (3) into current dollar terms by applying the increase in the US wholesale price index actually experienced during the period examined (1980–84). Thus, the baseline simulation for 1980–84 applies actual nominal changes in the dollar-yen rate to (2) and the actual values of the variables of (1) and (3), as well as the actual values of the real exchange rate $R^*_{YPD,t}$ (shown in table 2.7, chapter 2), to obtain the simulated actual 1980–84 trade experience (table 2.7, "actual: equation"). The simulation of hypothetical experience under different (equilibrium) exchange rates then applies the changed values of the underlying variables to the same set of equations. One additional equation is required to obtain the relative import price variable under hypothetical conditions:

(4) $P_t = P_{t-1}(1 + \dot{p}^s_{J,t} - \dot{p}^{WPI}_{U,t})$.

That is, the percentage change in the real price of imports facing US importers *equals* the percentage change in the dollar price of imports from Japan *less* the percentage change in US domestic wholesale prices. In the simulation of the cases using the hypothetical exchange rate, the hypothetical rates in table 2.5 are applied directly to the export equation (3a), and the nominal exchange rates corresponding to the new real exchange rates (for use in calculating the dollar price of Japan's exports, equations (2) and (2a)) are calculated based on the ratio of the hypothetical real exchange rates to the actual real exchange rates.

The simulation model does not incorporate the secondary effects of feedback from a change in the exchange rate to domestic inflation in either country. The terms $\dot{p}^{WPI}_{U,t}$ and $\dot{p}^d_{J,t}$ are treated exogenously and left at their original values in the hypothetical simulation cases. These secondary effects should be minor. For the United States, induced domestic price increases from depreciation of the trade-weighted exchange rate are generally believed to be approximately 0.15 times the amount of the depreciation, and to occur with a lag. In the case of Japan, the exchange rate change in the hypothetical case would be considerably smaller on a trade-weighted basis than in the yen-dollar rate, because only the United States is assumed to depreciate its currency.

Because the sharp rise in US imports from Japan in recent years has been the principal cause of the rising bilateral trade deficit, it is useful to consider in greater detail the underlying economic forces behind the increases in imports. Table B-1 presents a decomposition of the import increases into their component parts, based on the simulation model developed in this

TABLE B-1 **Decomposition of predicted increases in US imports from Japan, 1981–84**

Variable	Symbol	Elasticity in import equations[a]	Percentage change in variable			
			1981	1982	1983	1984
Real import price						
Current	P_t	−1.272	−4.66	−9.86	−2.64	−1.76
Lagged	P_{t-1}	−0.848	−8.05	−4.66	−9.86	−2.64
US income	Y_t	0.679	2.52	−2.13	3.70	6.81
Cyclical activity						
United States	A_{Ut}	1.622	−0.20	−4.73	1.06	4.08
Japan	$A_{J,t}$	−1.686	0.52	0.00	0.10	3.18
Industrial capacity, Japan	C_t	1.148	1.00	0.30	3.55	11.06
Cross-exchange rate, Japan	Z_t	0.147	−4.34	12.03	−3.77	−2.43
Compound effect	M_t^q	n.a.	n.a.	n.a.	n.a.	n.a.
Import price (predicted)	$P_{m,t}$	n.a.	2.60	−8.14	2.60	−0.42
Compound effect, value	M_t^v	n.a.	n.a.	n.a.	n.a.	n.a.
Memorandum item Actual change						
Volume	M_t^q	n.a.	n.a.	n.a.	n.a.	n.a.
Price	$P_{m,t}$	n.a.	n.a.	n.a.	n.a.	n.a.
Value	M_t^v	n.a.	n.a.	n.a.	n.a.	n.a.

n.a. Not applicable.
Source: Authors' calculations.
a. Equations (1c) and (2).
b. Equals percentage change in variable *times* elasticity.

Contribution to import increase (percentage)[b]			
1981	*1982*	*1983*	*1984*
5.93	12.54	3.36	2.24
6.83	3.95	8.36	2.24
1.71	− 1.45	2.51	4.62
− 0.32	− 7.67	1.72	6.62
− 0.88	0.00	− 0.17	− 5.36
1.15	0.34	4.08	12.70
− 0.64	1.77	− 0.55	− 0.36
15.23	10.43	21.73	24.43
2.60	− 8.14	2.60	− 0.42
18.23	1.44	24.93	23.89
16.32	8.81	10.66	37.76
4.04	− 8.04	− 1.42	0.60
21.00	0.08	9.09	38.59

appendix. The discussion of chapter 3 notes the principal developments behind the import increases in each phase of the period 1981–84, based on the details presented in table B-1.

The import and export equations presented here shed light on an ongoing controversy initiated by Houthakker and Magee in the 1960s.[5] Their trade equations indicated that the income elasticity for US imports substantially exceeded the income elasticities of US trading partners for imports from the United States. Subsequent analysts have argued that this asymmetry disappears once allowance is made for outward-shifting foreign supply and improving quality of foreign exports.[6] However, some subsequent studies appear to have again found a higher elasticity of US imports from Japan than of Japanese imports from the United States.[7]

An important recent study by Haynes and Stone finds that, in examining the symmetry of income elasticities, it is essential to distinguish between long-term (secular) income and short-term cyclical income elasticities.[8] The statistical estimates of this appendix appear to confirm the importance of

---

5. H. S. Houthakker and Stephen P. Magee, "Income and Price Elasticities in World Trade," *Review of Economics and Statistics,* vol. 51 (May 1969).

6. Bela Balassa, "Export Composition and Export Performance in the Industrial Countries, 1953–71," *Review of Economics and Statistics,* vol. 61, no. 4 (November 1979), pp. 604–7.

7. The Federal Reserve's Multi-country Model finds an income elasticity of 3.13 for US imports from Japan and 0.93 for Japan's imports from the United States. Guy V. G. Stevens, et al., *The U.S. Economy in an Interdependent World: A Multicountry Model* (Washington: Board of Governors of the Federal Reserve System, 1984), p. 131.

8. Using the statistical technique of spectral analysis, Haynes and Stone find the long-term income elasticity of US imports is 1.46, while the cyclical elasticity is 2.02. The long-term elasticity is considerably lower than a simple income elasticity that does not separate out cyclical effects (1.88). Moreover, in the Haynes–Stone results, the secular income elasticity of foreign demand for US exports is 1.50—virtually the same as the US import elasticity, and the Houthakker–Magee elasticity disparity disappears. Stephen E. Haynes and Joe A. Stone, "Secular and Cyclical Responses of U.S. Trade to Income: An Evaluation of Traditional Models," *Review of Economics and Statistics,* vol. 65, no. 1 (February 1983), pp. 87–95.

Evidence that the US import elasticity with respect to income is not higher than that of Japan is given more directly in the IMF's world trade model, which estimates the cyclical elasticity (for demand relative to potential output) at 2.17 for Japan's imports and only 1.22 for US imports (although the model imposes by assumption an equal elasticity of unity for long-term income effects). Grant H. Spencer, "The World Trade Model: Revised Estimates," *IMF Staff Papers,* vol. 31, no. 3 (September 1984), pp. 469–98.

distinguishing between the cyclical and secular income elasticities, as well as the view that outward-shifting supply has played a major role in Japan's export growth. With these two types of income effects separated and the term for Japan's industrial capacity included, the income elasticities are remarkably similar on both sides of US-Japan bilateral trade. The US secular income elasticity is 0.68 while the Japanese elasticity is 0.78; the US cyclical income elasticity is 1.62 while the Japanese elasticity is 1.81. Even the two countries' respective import elasticities with respect to the cyclical state of the other's economy are close in magnitude: −1.69 for US imports, and −2.20 for Japanese imports. In sum, the results here confirm that, after appropriate distinction between secular and cyclical income effects, there is no apparent asymmetry between the income elasticities of US imports from Japan and Japanese imports from the United States.

Two final implications of the estimates here warrant further discussion. First, these results indicate that exchange rate correction does have substantial impact on the US-Japan trade balance. A 10 percent depreciation of the dollar reduces the current dollar value of US imports from Japan by an estimated 9.4 percent, as discussed above. Applied to 1984 imports of $60 billion, this cutback is approximately $5.6 billion, or $560 million per percentage point of depreciation. On the export side, from equation (3) a 10 percent depreciation of the dollar causes an increase of 11.6 percent in the volume of US exports to Japan. (The value increase is the same, under the assumption that US export prices are determined by domestic wholesale prices and that feedback from dollar depreciation to these prices is sufficiently small to be omitted from the calculation.) Applied to the 1984 base of US exports to Japan ($24 billion), this relationship means that a 10 percent depreciation of the dollar relative to the yen causes an increase of $2.7 billion, or $270 million per percentage point. For the trade balance in current dollar terms, then, each percentage point depreciation in the dollar relative to the yen increases the bilateral balance by $830 million.

A second implication of the estimates is that although the Houthakker–Magee asymmetry on income elasticities is not found directly, there could nonetheless be secular pressure on the US trade balance with Japan. In the Houthakker–Magee formulation such pressure could arise because the income elasticity of US imports exceeds that of its exports, implying that unless US growth is lower than that abroad the trade balance will deteriorate. In the formulation here, no such disparity in income elasticities exists. However, long-term pressure in the trade balance could still arise from the supply-side effect identified here for Japan's exports to the United States. Specifically, a 1 percent rise in Japan's industrial capacity leads to an increase of 1.15 percent in Japan's exports to the United States. At unchanged prices and a constant exchange rate, and with both economies at normal capacity, long-term growth of 3 percent in the United States and 4.8 percent in Japan would cause US imports from Japan to grow at 7.6 percent annually ($0.68 \times 3 = 2.04$ percent from US income, *plus* $1.15 \times 4.8 = 5.52$ percent from outward-shifting Japanese supply), assuming that Japan's industrial capacity grows at the same rate as GNP. In contrast, Japan's demand for imports from the United States would grow at 3.7 percent annually (0.78×4.8 percent). However, for the future, the supply-shifting effect of Japanese growth might be less pronounced than in 1960–84, because the rapid pace of technical change in that period when the Japanese economy was catching up to the United States technologically might not be sustained by a Japan at the technological frontier. Otherwise, a one-time correction of the present overvaluation of the dollar might eventually have to be followed by small but steady annual appreciation of the yen relative to the dollar to maintain external equilibrium.[9]

---

9. Treating the trade bases as balanced between exports and imports—after dollar correction and incorporating the indirect effects on US export demand from third countries, given the triangular nature of the US-Japan trade relationship—differential supply-demand growth by a net amount of 3.9 percent annually would be offset by a secular appreciation of the yen relative to the dollar by about 2 percent annually. (With a net value elasticity of 0.94 on the import side and 0.78 on the export side for the United States, each percentage point appreciation of the dollar would generate an adjustment of about 1.7 percent of import value.) In terms of the trade-weighted exchange rate, any such secular appreciation of the yen (or depreciation of the dollar) would be considerably smaller.

Selected Bibliography

American Chamber of Commerce in Japan. 1982. "Report on 1981/82 Trade-Investment Barrier Membership Survey." ACCJ Position Papers. Tokyo, 8 March. Processed.

―――. 1982. "US-Japan Trade and Investment." ACCJ Position Papers. Prepared for presentation in Washington, 18–22 May. Processed.

Arthur D. Little, Inc. 1979. *The Japanese Non-Tariff Trade Barrier Issue: American Views and Implications for Japan-US Trade Relations.* Cambridge, Mass.

Balassa, Bela. 1984. "Intra-Industry Specialization: A Multi-Country Perspective." World Bank Discussion Paper No. DRD82. Washington, June.

―――. 1984. *Trends in International Trade in Manufactured Goods and Structural Change in the Industrial Countries.* World Bank Staff Working Paper No. 611. Washington.

Balassa, Bela, and Carol Balassa. 1984. "Industrial Protection in Developed Countries." *The World Economy,* vol. 7, no. 2, June.

Bergsten, C. Fred. 1977. *Managing International Economic Interdependence: Selected Papers of C. Fred Bergsten: 1975–1976.* Lexington, Mass.: D.C. Heath and Co.

―――. 1982. "What to Do About the U.S.-Japan Economic Conflict." *Foreign Affairs* (Summer), pp. 1059–75.

―――. 1984. "The Case for Leaning with the Wind." *Financial Times,* 24 October.

Bergsten, C. Fred, and John Williamson. 1983. "Exchange Rates and Trade Policy." In *Trade Policy in the 1980s.* Edited by William R. Cline. Washington: Institute for International Economics.

―――. 1986. *The Multiple Reserve Currency System.* Washington: Institute for International Economics, forthcoming.

Borrus, Michael, James Millstein, and John Zysman. 1982. *International Competition in Advanced Industrial Sectors: Trade and Development in the Semiconductor Industry.* Report prepared for the Joint Economic Committee. 97 Cong., 2 sess. Washington.

Capra, James, and Allen Sinai. 1985. "Deficit Prospects—Half Empty or Half Full?" *Economic Study Series,* no. 14. New York: Shearson Lehman Brothers, October.

Caves, Richard, and Masu Uekusa. 1976. "Industrial Organization." In *Asia's New Giant: How the Japanese Economy Works.* Edited by Hugh Patrick and Henry Rosovsky. Washington: Brookings Institution.

Chira, Susan. 1985. "Can U.S. Goods Succeed in Japan?" *New York Times,* 7 April.

Cline, William R. 1982. *"Reciprocity": A New Approach to World Trade Policy?* POLICY ANALYSES IN INTERNATIONAL ECONOMICS 2. Washington: Institute for International Economics, September.

―――. 1984. *Exports of Manufactures from Developing Countries: Performance and Prospects for Market Access.* Washington: Brookings Institution.

―――. 1984. "U.S. Trade and Industrial Policy: The Experience of Textiles, Steel, and Automobiles." Paper presented at the Export–Import Bank 50th Anniversary Conference, "Trade '84." Washington, October 25–26. Processed.

Congressional Budget Office (CBO). 1984. *The Effects of Import Quotas on the Steel Industry.* Washington, July.

167

———. 1985. *The Economic and Budget Outlook: An Update*. Washington, August.

Council of Economic Advisers. 1985. *Economic Report of the President 1985*. Washington, February.

Frankel, Jeffrey A. 1984. *The Yen/Dollar Agreement: Liberalizing Japanese Capital Markets*. POLICY ANALYSES IN INTERNATIONAL ECONOMICS 9. Washington: Institute for International Economics, December.

General Agreement on Tariffs and Trade (GATT) Secretariat. 1984. *International Trade 1983/ 84*. Geneva.

Goldstein, Morris, and Mohsin S. Khan. 1983. "Income and Price Effects in International Trade." In *Handbook of International Economics*. Edited by Peter B. Kenen and Ronald W. Jones. Amsterdam: North Holland Press.

Government-Ruling Parties, Joint Headquarters for the Promotion of External Economic Measures. 1985. *The Outline of the Action Program for Improved Market Access*. Tokyo, 30 July. Processed.

Hosomi, Takashi, and Mitsuhiro Fukao. 1985. *A Second Look at Foreign Exchange Market Interventions*. Tokyo: Japan Center for International Finance, April.

Hufbauer, Gary Clyde, and Jeffrey J. Schott. 1985. *Trading for Growth: The Next Round of Trade Negotiations*. POLICY ANALYSES IN INTERNATIONAL ECONOMICS 11. Washington: Institute for International Economics, September.

Hyde, Herbert F. (President, Burroughs of Japan and the American Chamber of Commerce in Japan). 1985. "US-Japan Trade Tensions: The View of American Business in Japan." Statement before the Japan-American Society of Washington, 4 June.

Industrial Bank of Japan. 1984. *Quarterly Review*, January–March.

Japan Economic Institute. 1984. *Yearbook of U.S.-Japan Economic Relations in 1983*. Washington.

Johnson, Chalmers. 1982. *MITI and the Japanese Miracle: The Growth of Industrial Policy, 1925–1975*. Stanford, Calif.: Stanford University Press.

Keidanren. 1985. "Smoothing the Way for Imports: Keidanren Presses for Regulatory Reform." Keizai Koho Center Brief No. 26. Tokyo, February.

Komiya, Ryutaro, and Miyako Suda. 1983. *Contemporary International Finance: Theory, History and Policy*. Tokyo: Nihon Keizai Shinbunsha.

Krause, Lawrence. 1985. Statement before the US House of Representatives. Subcommittee on International Economic Policy and Trade. Hearings on US-Japan Trade Relations. 99 Cong., 2 sess., 9 May.

Kravis, Irving B., Alan W. Heston, and Robert Summers. 1978. "Real GDP *Per Capita* for More Than One Hundred Countries." *Economic Journal*, vol. 88, no. 350 (June), pp. 215–42.

Krugman, Paul R. 1984. "The US Response to Foreign Industrial Targeting." *Brookings Papers on Economic Activity*, no. 1. Washington: Brookings Institution.

Loopesko, Bonnie E. 1984. "Relationships Among Exchange Rates, Intervention and Interest Rates: An Empirical Investigation." *Journal of International Money and Finance*, December.

Marris, Stephen. 1985. *Deficits and the Dollar: The World Economy at Risk*. POLICY ANALYSES IN INTERNATIONAL ECONOMICS 14. Washington: Institute for International Economics, December.

Noguchi, Yukio. 1985. "Tax Structure and Savings-Investment Balance." Paper presented to the US-Japan Consultative Group on International Monetary Affairs. Hakone, Japan, 25–26 April.

Nogués, Julio J., Andrzej Olechowski, and L. Alan Winters. 1985. "The Extent of Non-Tariff Barriers to Industrial Countries' Imports." World Bank Discussion Paper DRD115. Washington, January.

Nomura Research Institute. 1985. "A Long-Term Outlook for the Japanese Economy (Fiscal 1984 to 1995)." Tokyo, 26 August.

Nukazawa, Kazuo. 1985. "Keiretsu: Myths and Realities." Tokyo: Keidanren. Processed.

Ohmae, Kenichi. 1985. *Triad Power: The Coming Shape of Global Competition.* New York: Free Press.

Okumura, Hirohiko. 1985. "Japanese Portfolio Investments in Foreign Securities." Paper presented to the US-Japan Consultative Group on International Monetary Affairs. Hakone, Japan, 25–26 April.

Petri, Peter A. 1984. *Modeling Japanese–American Trade: A Study of Asymmetric Interdependence.* Cambridge, Mass.: Harvard University Press.

Reich, Michael R., Yasuo Endo, and C. Peter Timmer. 1985. "The Political Economy of Structural Change: Conflict Between Japanese and United States Agricultural Policy." Cambridge, Mass.: Harvard University, 25 June. Processed.

Rousch, Calvin T., Jr. 1984. *The Benefits of Eliminating the Alaskan Crude Oil Export Ban.* Washington: Federal Trade Commission, August.

Samuelson, Robert J. 1985. "Messy Trade Problems." *Washington Post,* 28 August.

Saxonhouse, Gary R. 1983. "What Is All This About 'Industrial Targeting' in Japan?" *The World Economy,* vol. 6 (September), pp. 253–74.

————. 1983. "The Micro- and Macroeconomics of Foreign Sales to Japan." In *Trade Policy in the 1980s.* Edited by William R. Cline. Washington: Institute for International Economics.

Sazanami, Yoko. 1981. "Possibilities of Expanding Intra-Industry Trade in Japan." *Keio Economic Studies,* vol. 18, no. 2.

Scott, Bruce R. 1985. "US Competitiveness: Concepts, Performance, and Implications." In *US Competitiveness in the World Economy.* Edited by Bruce R. Scott and George C. Lodge. Boston, Mass.: Harvard Business School Press.

————. "National Strategies." In *U.S. Competitiveness in the World Economy.* Edited by Bruce R. Scott and George C. Lodge. Boston, Mass.: Harvard Business School Press.

Semiconductor Industry Association. 1985. *Japanese Market Barriers in Microelectronics.* San Jose, Calif., 14 June.

Staiger, Robert W., Alan V. Deardorff, and Robert M. Stern. 1985. "The Effects of Protection on the Factor Content of Japanese and American Foreign Trade." Ann Arbor: University of Michigan, 29 March. Processed.

Tarr, David G., and Morris E. Morkre. 1984. *Aggregate Costs to the United States of Tariffs and Quotas on Imports: General Tariff Cuts and Removal of Quotas on Automobiles, Steel, Sugar, and Textiles.* Washington: Federal Trade Commission, December.

US General Accounting Office. 1979. *United States–Japan Trade: Issues and Problems.* Washington.

US International Trade Commission. 1983. *Foreign Industrial Targeting and the Effects on US Industries. Phase I. Japan.* USITC Publication No. 1437. Washington, October.

————. 1985. *US Imports of Textile and Apparel Products under the Multifiber Arrangement, January–June 1984*. USITC Publication No. 1635. Washington, January.

————. 1985. *The Automobile Industry: Monthly Report on Selected Economic Indicators*. USITC Publication No. 1650. Washington, February.

————. 1985. *Monthly Report on Selected Steel Industry Data*. USITC Publication No. 1700. Washington, May.

US Trade Representative. 1985. "US Statement on Japanese Market Access." Addressed to OECD Trade Commitee. Washington, 11 June.

Vogel, Ezra. 1985. *Comeback Case by Case: Building the Resurgence of American Business*. New York: Simon and Schuster.

Wallich, Henry C., and Mable I. Wallich. 1976. "Banking and Finance." In *Asia's New Giant: How the Japanese Economy Works*. Edited by Hugh Patrick and Henry Rosovsky. Washington: Brookings Institution.

Walter, Ingo. 1984. "Structural Adjustment and Trade Policy in the International Steel Industry." In *Trade Policy in the 1980s*. Edited by William R. Cline. Washington: Institute for International Economics.

Williamson, John. 1985. *The Exchange Rate System*. POLICY ANALYSES IN INTERNATIONAL ECONOMICS 5. 2d ed., rev. Washington: Institute for International Economics, June.

Yoshitomi, Masaru. 1985. *Japan as Capital Exporter and the World Economy*. Occasional Paper No. 18. New York: Group of Thirty.

————. 1986. "Japan's View of Current External Imbalances." In *Global Economic Imbalances*. Edited by C. Fred Bergsten. Washington: Institute for International Economics, March.

Other Publications from the Institute

POLICY ANALYSES IN INTERNATIONAL ECONOMICS SERIES

BOOKS

Economic Sanctions Reconsidered: History and Current Policy
Gary Clyde Hufbauer and Jeffrey J. Schott, assisted by Kimberly Ann Elliott/
1985

Trade Protection in the United States: 31 Case Studies
*Gary Clyde Hufbauer, Diane T. Berliner, and Kimberly Ann Elliott/*1986

Toward Renewed Economic Growth in Latin America
*Bela Balassa, Gerardo M. Bueno, Pedro-Pablo Kuczynski, and Mario Henrique
Simonsen/*1986

American Trade Politics: System Under Stress
*I.M. Destler/*1986

SPECIAL REPORTS

1 Promoting World Recovery: A Statement on Global Economic Strategy *by
   Twenty-six Economists from Fourteen Countries/*December 1982

2 Prospects for Adjustment in Argentina, Brazil, and Mexico: Responding to
   the Debt Crisis
   *John Williamson, editor/*June 1983

3 Inflation and Indexation: Argentina, Brazil, and Israel
   *John Williamson, editor/*March 1985

4 Global Economic Imbalances
   *C. Fred Bergsten, editor/*March 1986

5 African Debt and Financing
   *Carol Lancaster and John Williamson, editors/*May 1986

FORTHCOMING

United States–Canadian Interdependence: The Quest for Free Trade
Paul Wonnacott

Capital Flight and Third World Debt
Donald R. Lessard and John Williamson

Auction Quotas and US Trade Policy
C. Fred Bergsten and Jeffrey J. Schott

The Future of World Trade in Textiles and Apparel
William R. Cline

Agriculture and the GATT: Issues in a New Trade Round
Dale E. Hathaway

The United States as a Debtor Country
C. Fred Bergsten and Shafiqul Islam

Domestic Adjustment and International Trade
Gary Clyde Hufbauer and Howard F. Rosen, editors

Target Zones and Policy Coordination
Marcus Miller and John Williamson